Practise Your ENGLISH

Intermediate to First Certificate

W. S. Fowler   **Norman Coe**

Nelson

Contents

Modals and auxiliaries

Verb forms

INTRODUCTION

Most students find practice exercises dull, especially if they have to do with grammatical points they have already learned and believe they understand. At the same time, as your English improves, you realise that you are not always sure why you have been corrected and would like a clear explanation so that you won't make the same mistake again.

The exercises in this book are designed to correct errors commonly made by students at your level of English. As far as possible, we have tried to make them interesting, as well as giving you model sentences showing how the language works in given situations, and brief grammatical explanations to clear up points that may confuse you.

What is new about these exercises, however, is that they are mainly designed to be used with the *Test Your English* series, which helps you to find out what your weaknesses are. The test items are linked to the exercises by means of a cross-reference index in the *Test Your English* Teacher's Guide and in the Answer Keys to *Practise Your English*. In this way, the exercises you will need to do will only be those relating to grammatical points which you, or the class as a whole, have shown you are uncertain about in the test. This saves a great deal of valuable time since you or the teacher can concentrate on the points that clearly need attention.

We trust that in this way you will find work with practice exercises more interesting and more useful than it has been up to now.

W S Fowler
Norman Coe
Barcelona, October 1981

Determiners

1 **a/an** with expressions of frequency

Notice how **a** is used in the following answer:

    A   How often do you go to the theatre?
    B   About twice **a** month.

We use **a** or **an** in expressions of frequency to answer questions like **how much**, **how many**, **how fast**, etc. **Twice a month** means 'twice in one month'.

Choose the expression on the right which best answers each question on the left:

1 How often do you shave?	a Twice a year.
2 How fast can you run?	b Eighty beats a minute.
3 How often do you have examinations?	c Three times a week.
	d Twenty km. an hour.
4 How much do you smoke?	e Thirty cigarettes a day.
5 What is your pulse rate?	f Once a day.
6 How often do you have English classes?	

2 **all** and **every** with expressions of time

Compare these sentences:

    I haven't seen him **all day**. (since I got up this morning)
    He goes to work **every day** except Sundays.

With periods of time (day, week, etc.) **all** refers to the total period of time (duration), **every** to a period of time which is continually repeated.

Complete these sentences with **all** or **every**:

1   The neighbours had a party until five o'clock this morning. It kept me awake _____ night.
2   Each morning just before dawn, the birds start singing outside my bedroom window. They wake me up _____ morning.
3   Evergreen trees are called 'evergreen' because they keep their leaves _____ year.
4   In America, autumn is called 'fall' because it is the time when the leaves fall from the trees _____ year.
5   The programme is shown from 7.00 to 8.00 _____ Sunday evening.
6   The film was four hours long. It lasted _____ Sunday evening.
7   In London, dustmen come to collect the rubbish _____ week.
8   The shop said they were sending a man to mend the television on Monday, but we've been waiting _____ week for him and he still hasn't come.
9   _____ time we meet he says hello.
10   He has never said hello to me in _____ the time I've known him.

3 Use and omission of **the**

a Omission of **the**

We do <u>not</u> use **the** with the following:

1 Games and sports

I **play football** every week. My sister **plays tennis** and **likes swimming**, too.

Which games or sports are the following people famous for?
Mohammad Ali, Pele, Jack Nicklaus, Sebastian Coe, Nadia Comaneci,

e.g. **Bjorn Borg is famous for tennis.**

2 Subjects of study

I **studied literature** at university and now I **teach English**.

Which subject would you study if you were interested in the work of Shakespeare, Sophocles, Einstein, Mozart, Keynes, Pasteur?

e.g. **If I were interested in the work of Marconi, I would study physics.**

3 Languages

Many Welsh people **speak Welsh** but most Scots **speak English**.

Note that we can say **the English** (noun) or **English people**, but nationality as an adjective has no definite or indefinite article,

e.g. **I'm English.**

Which language do the following speak? – the Austrians, the Brazilians, the Danes, the Cretans, the Swiss,

e.g. **The Belgians speak French or Flemish.**

4 Meals and clock time

A What time do you **have breakfast**?
B **About eight o'clock.**

5 Gerunds

Horse racing is more popular in Britain than **fox-hunting**.

6 Collocations (preposition + noun)

Notice that there is no **the** after the preposition in these sentences:

e.g. Is he still **in bed**?
No, he's **at church**.
I was **at school** for thirteen years and then I went **to university**.

A number of common phrases in English made up of a preposition and a noun do not take **the**.

Here is a list of the most common ones:
bed (**in, to**)
church (**at, in** = inside, **to**)
court (**in, to**)
dock (**in**)
harbour (**in, to**)
home (**at**)
hospital (**in, to**)
market (**at, to**)
paper (**on**)
prison (**in, to**)
school (**at, to**)
sea (**at, to**)
university (**at, to**)
work (**at, to**)

The definite article is only used when we clearly refer to a particular school, hospital, etc.

e.g.   My mother's **in hospital**.
I'm going **to the hospital** this afternoon to take her some flowers.

Modes of travel and transport take **by** + noun, without **the**,

e.g.   **by air/sea/road**
by car/bus/plane/train, etc.

Note that we say **on foot**.

Use the list above to complete the following sentences with the correct preposition:

1   If you refuse to pay the fine, they will take you _____ court.
2   The children are _____ school, my husband's _____ work and I'm _____ home, cooking the dinner.
3   His ship's _____ dock after six months _____ sea.
4   Her mother always goes _____ church on Sundays, but she stays _____ bed.
5   Would you rather travel _____ sea or _____ air?
6   Most of the guests came _____ car but I came _____ foot.

b   Use of **the**
We use **the** with the following:

1   Weights and measures
Petrol is sold **by the litre**.

Match each commodity in List **A** with a suitable measure in List **B** and write a sentence, as in the example above, about each:

A		B	
1	land	a	metre
2	cloth	b	kilo
3	milk	c	hectare
4	sugar	d	litre

2 Groups or classes of people

The young often get impatient with their parents.

We can say either **the young** or **young people**. The verb that follows expressions of this kind is plural.

Match each group of people in List **A** with a suitable sentence ending from List **B** to form complete sentences, like the example above:

A		B	
1	The blind	a	haven't got much money.
2	The deaf	b	can learn to read Braille.
3	The lonely	c	may have to go to hospital.
4	The poor	d	have a lot of money.
5	The rich	e	need hearing aids.
6	The sick	f	have no friends.

3 Rivers, seas, mountain ranges

The Amazon is longer than **the River Thames**.
The Mediterranean flows into **the Atlantic Ocean**.
Mount Everest is the highest mountain in **the Himalayas**.

Note that we use **the** in all cases, except for the name of a single mountain, e.g. **Mount Everest, Kilimanjaro.**

4 Unique objects, points of the compass, some time expressions

The sun rises in **the east**.
The past is often more real to old people than **the present**.

We use **the** when there is only one of something, e.g. **the sun, the moon, the earth, the world**.
We use **the** with points of the compass, e.g. **the north, the south, the east, the west**. But compare these sentences:
We were travelling **north**.
We were travelling **towards the north**.

We usually use **the** when we speak of **the past, the present** and **the future**. The exceptions are **at present** which means 'now, at this time' and **in future** which means 'from now on',

e.g. I'll drive more carefully **in future**. (from now on, from this moment)
In the future (but not from now on) men may live on the moon.

c Use and omission of **the**

A good rule to remember is:
we use **the** when we are talking about something specific;
we don't use **the** when we are speaking in a more general sense.

1 Plural count nouns and mass nouns

She likes **flowers**. (general)
She liked **the flowers** that I gave her. (specific)
Coffee is expensive nowadays. (general)
The coffee that you bought is very bitter. (specific)

2 Abstract nouns

I always admire **honesty**. (general)
I was surprised at **the honesty** with which he answered the
questions. (specific)

3 Species of animals

Elephants are said to have long memories.

When we talk about animals in general, we usually use the plural without
the. When we refer to a particular species we can use *either* **the** and a
singular noun,

e.g. **The Indian elephant is smaller than the African elephant.**
or a plural noun without **the**,

e.g. **Indian elephants are smaller than African elephants.**

4 Noun + modifying phrase/clause

Life is always valuable.
Modern life is often tiring.
Albert Schweitzer's life was devoted to the sick.
The life of Albert Schweitzer was devoted to the sick.
The life he is leading bores him.
The life of our grandparents was very different from **the life we lead** today.

The is used when the noun is modified by a relative clause, or by a phrase
including **of**.

Put **the** where it is necessary in the following:

1 Tom is fond of _____ music.
2 Mozart composed _____ music in the eighteenth century.
3 She likes _____ music of the eighteenth century.
4 She likes _____ music that Mozart composed.
5 She likes _____ Mozart's music.
6 She likes _____ music of Mozart.
7 She prefers _____ classical music to _____ pop music.
8 I don't think _____ music we heard on the radio last night was
really _____ jazz. It didn't sound like _____ Louis Armstrong's
music, though some of _____ music of the 1920s, _____ music
they played in New Orleans, was a bit like it.

4   a lot of, a great/good deal of, a large amount/number of

Look at these sentences:

> He's done **a lot of** work.
> He's done **a great deal of** work.
> **A lot of** money was stolen from the bank.
> **A large amount of** money was stolen from the bank.
> **A lot of** people came to the wedding.
> **A large number of** people came to the wedding.

A lot of can be used with mass nouns and with plural count nouns.
In the affirmative we tend to use it rather than **much** or **many**.
But compare the negative:

He hasn't done much work.
Not many people came to the party.

A great deal of, **a good deal of** and **a large amount of** are used with mass nouns.

A large amount of is preferred to define the amount of a product, money, or something which can be measured fairly easily.

A (large) number of is only used with count nouns.

Use **a great deal of**, **a large amount of** or **a (large) number of** in place of **a lot of** in the following:

1   He took *a lot of* trouble to make the party a success. He invited *a lot of* people and bought *a lot of* food. In fact, there was *a lot of* food left over – enough to feed an army, so the next day he asked *a lot of* friends to come back and help him eat it.

2   This booklet offers *a lot of* useful information to young people who want to study in England. *A lot of* students go to England every year and there are *a lot of* courses to choose from, but students often waste *a lot of* time trying to find out which ones will suit them and whether they have right qualifications. This booklet will save them *a lot of* wasted effort.

3   *A*   I'd like to borrow £1000.
   B   That's *a lot of* money.
   A   Well, I have *a lot of* bills to pay.
   B   *A lot of* people come to the bank asking for loans but when they ask for such *a lot of* money, they usually offer guarantees.
   A   Well, I have *a lot of* friends. I'm sure they'll help.
   B   Then why don't you ask them for the money?
   A   To be honest, because I already owe a lot to *a lot of* them.

5 few, a few, little, a little

a a few and a little

Look at these sentences:

> I've bought **a few** flowers for your birthday.
> Would you like some milk? Yes, please. Just **a little**.

We use **a few** with count nouns and **a little** with mass nouns. Both have positive meaning, so **a few** means 'not many, but enough' and **a little** means 'not much, but enough'.

Complete the dialogue, using **a few** or **a little**:

Joan   What are you doing, Mum?

Mother I've invited __1__ friends to tea so I'm making __2__ cakes.

Joan   What do you put in them?

Mother Well, flour, of course, and then I mix it with __3__ butter and __4__ sugar, and I add __5__ raisins. Then I pour __6__ lemon juice on top. Grandma always pours in __7__ wine instead, and she adds __8__ cherries instead of the raisins, but I prefer raisins with this recipe.

Joan   What else are you going to give them?

Mother Well, I'll make __9__ sandwiches and there are __10__ biscuits in the tin. That should be enough.

b few and little

Look at these sentences:

> (Very) **Few** people like rats.
> He's very ill. There's (very) **little** hope that he will recover.

Both **few** and **little** have negative meaning, so **few** means 'not many' and **little** means 'not much'.

Complete the passage, using **few** or **little**:

Deserta is a poor country. It has __1__ natural resources and there is __2__ cultivable land. There are very __3__ towns and there is __4__ contact with other countries because there are __5__ good roads, __6__ navigable rivers, and there is very __7__ money available to import goods from abroad. Most of the people live in the country but there are __8__ farms and very __9__ farm animals. It is difficult to grow crops; the Desertans have __10__ corn or wheat and __11__ of them can afford to buy meat. Deserta receives very __12__ help from the outside world and __13__ governments are even aware that it exists. There is __14__ hope of any improvement in the situation unless Deserta receives foreign aid.

c **few, a few, little, a little**

Compare these sentences:

> I **don't think** there's **much** use trying to persuade him; he's already made up his mind.
>
> I **think** there's **little** use trying to persuade him; he's already made up his mind.

Rewrite these sentences, using **little**, **a little**, **few** or **a few**, as in the example above:

1 She worked hard, although her boss *didn't give* her *much* encouragement.
2 *Not many* people voted for him; he's not popular.
3 Would you like *some* sugar in your tea?
4 There have been *some* cases of stealing in the firm but *not many* workers were involved, and there is *not much* reason to be alarmed.
5 *A* You look as though you need *some* help.
   B Yes, there are *some* problems I don't understand.
6 *Not many* teachers think that students can learn English *without much* effort, though *some* suggest this to give the students *some* encouragement. Personally, I *don't see much* sense in saying that.

6 **most, most of**

Notice the use of **most** and **most of** in these sentences:

> **Most** bread is made from wheat. **Most** cakes contain sugar.
>
> **Most of** the cheese you bought was bad. **Most of** the cakes you made were burnt.

When we are speaking generally, **most** means 'the greatest part of' (with mass nouns) or 'the majority of' (with count nouns). When we are talking about particular cases, e.g. **the cakes you made**, **most of** means 'more than half of' the thing which we are referring to.

Use **most** or **most of** instead of the phrases in italics in the following exercise:

1 *The majority of* people get married, although *the majority of* men pretend that they are not really in favour of it. Curiously enough *the majority of* divorced people in Britain marry again. In fact, *more than half of* them get married again within a year or two of the divorce.
2 *The greater part of* work is boring and *the majority of* people do boring jobs, but unfortunately if they did not work so hard, they would spend *more than half of* their time doing nothing or watching television, *the greater part of* which is a waste of time, anyway.
3 When I started teaching, the *majority of* teachers said we should not talk about provocative subjects in class. The trouble is that *the*

majority of interesting subjects are provocative so *more than half of* the discussions we had were dull. But *more than half of* the younger generation of teachers believe in free discussion. This is all right, except that *the majority of* them seem to belong to political parties and spend *more than half of* their time trying to convert the students to their point of view.

7 wine bottle, bottle of wine

Compare the following sentences:

He bought a **packet of cigarettes**.
He threw the **cigarette packet** away.

A **cigarette packet** is empty, but a **packet of cigarettes** is full or has some cigarettes in it.
Similarly, **a wine bottle** is empty, but **a bottle of wine** is full or has some wine in it.
Note that the singular form is used when the noun is used as an adjective, even though it is a count noun (cigarette packet).

Which of the following would you give a friend as a present: **a case of champagne, a cigar box, a whisky bottle, a box of chocolates, a bottle of perfume?**

Correct the following sentences:

e.g.   I'm going to buy a whisky bottle.
I'm going to buy a bottle of whisky.

1   I'm going to wash up the cups of coffee.
2   We're going to have a lot of people staying with us next week, so I'd better get a potato sack.
3   Put the bottles of milk on the doorstep. The milkman will collect them.
4   Good heavens! Johnny has eaten a whole sweet bag.
5   What else do we need at the grocer's? Oh, yes, some fruit tins and a matchbox.

8   one, ones, the one, the ones

Notice the difference between **one** and **the one** in these sentences:

A   Would you like an orange?
B   Yes, I'd love **one**. (Any orange will do, I'm not asking for a particular one.)
A   Who's he?
B   He's **the one** who was so unpleasant to Julia last Saturday. (I'm identifying a specific person.)

We use the word **one** in a sentence to avoid repeating a count noun,

e.g.   **The uniform the children have chosen is one** (a uniform) **they all like.**
The best recipe for making jam is the one (the recipe) **my mother always uses.**
He bought collars for his two dogs. Sam wore a black one (collar) **and Jack a brown one** (collar).
Which glasses do you prefer – the green ones (glasses) **or the brown ones** (glasses)?

Complete these sentences with **one**, **ones**, **the one** or **the ones**:

1   I recognise that tune. It's _____ I'm very fond of.
2   That's Beethoven's Third Symphony; isn't it _____ they began *Concert Hour* with last night?
3   These strawberries are not as good as _____ we had yesterday.
4   We didn't have enough plates for the party, so we used paper _____ instead.
5   *A*   All the pieces she played were beautiful, of course, but which _____ did you like best?
    B   _____ she played last.

9   one ... another/the other, some ... others/the others

Compare these sentences:

At the meeting last week, **one** group was in favour of new elections; **another** preferred things to remain as they were; **a third** group said elections should be held after Christmas.
At the meeting last week, **some** people were in favour of new elections; **others** preferred things to remain as they were; **others** said elections should be held after Christmas.

I've got two boys. **One** of them is very cheerful but **the other** is often depressed.

She has six children. **Two** of them live at home, but **the others** have flats or houses of their own.

If only two people, things or groups of people or things are referred to, we use **the other** or **the others**.

Complete these sentences with **one, another, the other, some, others** or **the others**:

1   There are two main reasons why horses may not run as well as expected in races. _____ is that the horse may have been given drugs; _____ is that someone may have paid the jockey to ride badly.

2   Most people lose money betting on horse racing. _____ know nothing about horses; _____ know a lot but allow the need to gamble to affect their judgement.

3   All the girls in the school were wearing jeans, except two; _____ wore a blouse and skirt and _____ a dress.

4   Most of the boys wore jeans, too, but _____ wore trousers and _____ wore shorts.

5   They had three children, _____ was a boy and _____ were girls.

6   When the children grew up, _____ became a doctor, _____ an accountant and the third was a nurse.

7   These days _____ girls are more interested in a career than in getting married; _____ still look forward to having a large family; and there are _____, perhaps the majority, who would like to do both.

8   There is a proverb that suggests that _____ people hate what _____ like. The proverb is '_____ man's meat is _____ man's poison'.

NOTE   One other is used in sentences like this:

I have given you a number of reasons why I disagree with the proposal but there is **one other** I would like to mention before I sit down.

(It is an emphatic form of **another**, meaning 'only one'.)

Some others occurs in sentences like this:

We have received a number of letters from readers on this subject. The majority supported our point of view; others were against it, and there were **some others** that proposed a completely new approach.

(It is an emphatic form of **others**, implying 'a few others'.)

10 people, everyone, everything

a Subject/verb agreement

Notice whether the verb is singular or plural in these sentences:

He **is** a pleasant **person**. They **are** pleasant **people**.
Most **people like** animals.
Everyone likes to have a holiday.
Everything is ready.

The word **people** is always plural in English. We hardly ever use the form 'persons'.
On the other hand, **everyone (everybody)** and **everything** are always singular.
We never say 'all people' or 'all persons' and we hardly ever use the form 'all things'. 'All the people' and 'all the things' are not often used, either.

Put the verbs in brackets in the singular or the plural form, and choose between **he/they**:

1 Everything that (have) been done (be) useful.
2 Everyone who (know) him (like) him.
3 Most people (be) afraid of snakes.
4 People who (bet) on races are called punters.
5 It is surprising that people who (put) on special clothes when (he/they) (go) climbing (not do) the same thing when (he/they) (go) out in boats.
6 English people (drink) more than (he/they) used to.

b Possessive of **people** and **everyone**

Compare the use of the possessive adjectives in these sentences:

The people who work in the office have **their** own desks.
Everyone who works in the office has **his** own desk.

We use the plural possessive adjective, **their**, with **people**.
We use the singular possessive adjective, **his**, with **everyone**, unless we know that all the people concerned are women; then we use **her**.
Since **people** is a plural word, we can talk about **many people** and **a number of people**. We cannot use **much** or **a great deal of** with **people**.

Put **his** or **their** in each space, put the verbs in brackets in the singular or the plural form, and choose between **he/they** and **much/many**:

1 (Much/many) people (buy) suitcases to carry _____ luggage when (he/they) (go) abroad.
2 There (not be) (much/many) people there, and (he/they) (be) all very tired.
3 Everyone who (enter) for the competition must provide _____ own equipment.

4 English people, probably because of _____ holidays abroad, (drink) more wine nowadays, but (he/they) usually (not know) much about it. Still, as the French say, *Chacun à son goût* – Everyone to _____ own taste.

5 (Much/many) more people (die) from bee stings than snake bites in Britain, but everyone (think) snakes are more dangerous.

6 All the people who (come) to our parties enjoy (himself/themselves).

7 Everyone who (visit) the city (enjoy) (himself/themselves).

8 *A* Everyone (love) me.

   B Really? I know some people who (not do).

11   no one, none, any, someone, anyone

a   no one

Compare these sentences:

        They weren't invited.

        No one invited them.

Rewrite these sentences beginning **No one . . .**, as in the example above:

1 She wasn't asked to come.

2 We weren't paid for our work.

3 I wasn't given anything.

4 She isn't liked.

5 It wasn't stolen.

6 You weren't asked for your opinion.

7 I'm not going to be insulted.

8 They won't be punished.

9 We weren't forced to do it.

10 He hasn't been told the news.

b   none and any

Compare the use of **none** and **any** in this sentence:

        He **didn't speak** to **any** of us and **none** of us **spoke** to him.

We use **none** as a negative subject in a clause or a sentence. **None** means 'not one' and takes a singular verb in the affirmative.

Complete these sentences using **none** or **any**:

1 She wasn't interested in _____ of them and _____ of them was interested in her.

2 _____ of us liked him and he didn't like _____ of us, either.

3 _____ of us likes the family and _____ of them likes us.

4 I couldn't use _____ of them. _____ of them works.

5 I haven't taken _____ of your records. You won't find _____ of them here. _____ of them is worth listening to, anyway.

6 **A** _____ of his books is worth reading.

  B How do you know? You haven't read _____ of them.

  A Well, _____ of his friends likes them.

someone and **anyone**

Compare these sentences:

Listen! There's **someone** at the door.

It's not a difficult job. **Anyone** could do it.

Someone means 'a particular person', although perhaps we do not know his name; **anyone**, in an affirmative sentence, means 'a person, any person, whoever he is and whatever he is like'.

Complete these sentences using **someone** or **anyone**:

Doris	He's an impossible man, and ___1___ should tell him so.
Flo	Ssh! ___2___ may hear you.
Doris	I don't care. ___3___ would say the same in my situation.
Doris	Oh, ___4___ rang while you were out.
Mr Cross	Who was it?
Doris	I don't know. I didn't ask him.
Mr Cross	Good heavens! ___5___ with a little common sense would have taken a message. It may have been ___6___ important.
Doris	Well, if it was, I expect he'll ring back.
Mr Cross	Miss Smith, ___7___ but you would have asked him his name. That's what I pay you for. ___8___ could do a simple job like yours.
Doris	Well, you'd better look for ___9___ then, Mr Cross, because I'm leaving. But your wife might like to know that you took ___10___ out to lunch today, ___11___ called Gloria from the accounts office.
Mr Cross	Now, Miss Smith, er, Doris, don't get upset. ___12___ can lose his temper, you know.

12   **someone else, something else,** etc.

Notice the use of **else** in these sentences:

  A Who broke this window?

  B I didn't. **Someone else** did.

  A Who went to Sue's party?

  B John and Martin did.

A Did **anyone else** go?
B Yes, Jack and Jill. **No one else** was invited.
A Do we need **anything else**?
B No, **nothing else**. Just a minute, we do need some sugar. I've got **everything else**.

Else is a singular form meaning 'other person' or 'other thing'. Note that in the plural we say 'other people' or 'other things'.
Else is also used with question words,

e.g. **Who else came to the party?**
What else did they say?
How else (in what other way) **do you expect me to do it?**

The possessive is **else's**,

e.g. **This watch isn't mine. It's someone else's.**

Complete these sentences with **else** and the word in brackets, together with **any**, **no**, **some** or **every** where necessary:

e.g. That's all, thank you. I don't need (thing).
That's all, thank you. I don't need anything else.

1 I'm only interested in having a good time; (thing) matters.
2 *A* Only you would behave like that; (one) would have more sense.
  B That's not true. You think (one) thinks like you.
3 While you were out, Jim rang. And (one) else rang too, but he didn't give his name. He just asked for you. He didn't say (thing).
4 *A* Whose is this pen? Is it yours?
  B No, it must be (one's). It's a ballpoint. I'm the only person in the office who still uses a fountain pen. (one) uses a ballpoint.
5 *A* (What) can I do to help?
  B There's (thing) to do. I've laid the table and (thing) is ready in the kitchen.
  A That's all right, then. To be honest, I don't like interfering with the arrangements in (one's) house.
  B No, of course not. You can help me with the washing-up afterwards, though. (one) will want to do that.

13 Reflexive pronouns: **myself**, etc.; **each other, one another**

a Reflexive verbs
Notice the reflexive verbs in these sentences:

He didn't have a guitar teacher. He **taught himself**.

I **looked at myself** in the mirror this morning and **said to myself**, 'You need a holiday.'
The children **enjoyed themselves** very much.

The following verbs are often found in reflexive constructions:
a   verbs connected with action, pain or danger: **burn, cut, defend, drown, hurt, kill, shoot.**
b   verbs connected with behaviour or emotion: **amuse, behave, blame, control, deceive, enjoy, be ashamed of, be sorry for, feel sorry for.**
c   verbs connected with thought or speech: **consider, count, express, say to, talk to, tell, think.**
    Count and **think** are often reflexive when they have the meaning of 'consider',

e.g. **Count/Think yourself lucky that you escaped.**

d   verbs indicating actions which are not normally reflexive: **congratulate, educate, introduce, invite, teach.**
e   other verbs: **can't help, prevent, stop, weigh.**

Use each of the following verbs in the correct form <u>once only</u> followed by a suitable reflexive pronoun to complete these sentences:

be ashamed of, behave, enjoy, feel sorry for, introduce, talk to, teach, weigh

1   She's frightened of getting fat so she _____ every morning.
2   When people _____, they say it's a sign that they are going mad.
3   I _____ very much at the party. I had a wonderful time.
4   He speaks several languages. He's _____ Portuguese now.
5   Daddy says we can stay up to watch the programme on TV if we _____.
6   Oh, do stop _____. A lot of other people in the world are unhappy, too.
7   No one spoke to her so she went up to various people and _____.
8   You ought to _____. I've never seen such badly behaved children.

b   Verbs with reflexive sense but not form

Notice the absence of the reflexive pronoun in these sentences:
Elaine and I **got engaged** last week and we're **getting married** in the summer.
She **apologised** for being late and **sat down** near the back of the class.

A number of verbs in English, reflexive in some other languages, employ **get** instead: **get accustomed to, get confused, get dressed, get engaged, get excited, get lost, get married, get tired, get upset, get wet.**

There is also a group, reflexive in some other languages, where in English the use of the reflexive pronoun is not necessary or is incorrect: **apologise (for), bathe, decide, fall asleep, find out, forget, get up** (rise), **hide, hurry, improve** (get better), **join, move, prepare (for), remember, resign** (from a job), **retire** (from work), **shave, sit down, stand up, wake up, wash, wonder, worry.**

Use each of the following verbs in the correct form once only to complete these sentences. Do not use a reflexive pronoun.

bathe, decide, get up, hurry, resign, retire, shave, wash, wonder, worry

1 He _____ very early every morning and goes into the bathroom to _____ and _____ before breakfast.
2 His mother had told him not to _____ in the sea because he couldn't swim.
3 *A* _____! We'll miss the train.
   B Don't _____. We've still got plenty of time.
4 I'm so fed up with my boss that I'm going to _____. I'm not going to stay in this firm until I _____ at the age of 65.
5 I _____ why they have offered me the job. I'm not really very experienced. Anyway, I _____ to accept it.

c **each other** and **one another**

Notice that **each other** and **one another** have the same meaning:
   They love **each other** and they're going to get married.
   They love **one another** and they're going to get married.

Rewrite the following sentences, changing one form to the other, as in the examples above:

1 We always feel sad when we have to say goodbye to each other.
2 They're always arguing with one another.
3 When two people love each other, they usually manage to solve their problems.
4 Some married couples never talk to each other in public.
5 I was just going to introduce you. I didn't realise you already knew one another.

d **myself, yourself,** etc. and **each other, one another**

Compare these sentences:
   When you look in a mirror you see **yourself.**
   You and your friend can talk to **each other/one another** on the telephone.

Alan sees himself in a mirror means that Alan sees Alan.
Alan and Bill talk to each other means that Alan talks to Bill, and Bill talks to Alan.

Complete the following sentences with a reflexive pronoun or **each other/one another**:

1 Parents often complain that television stops children amusing _____ with creative games.
2 They told _____ jokes to pass the time.
3 The two sisters are very fond of _____ and if anyone criticises either of them they always defend _____.
4 The three of us were attacked by a group of thugs in the street so we had to defend _____.
5 Don't blame _____ for what happened. It wasn't your fault, Tony, and it wasn't Joan's fault, either. I don't want you to argue with _____ about it.
6 I've always wanted to meet you but we've never had the chance to talk to _____ until now. Let me introduce _____. My name's Alan.

14 Reflexive pronoun used for emphasis

Look at these sentences:

I'm not going to do it for you. Do it **yourself**!
The Queen **herself** gave it to me.

The reflexive pronouns here emphasise the words they go with.

Use the appropriate reflexive pronoun to make the sentences below emphatic, in the same way as the examples above:

1 I wouldn't take any notice of you even if you were the king _____.
2 Why should they expect us to do it for them? They ought to do it _____.
3 Would you mind taking these letters to the post? I haven't got time to do it _____.
4 Cynthia Jones is getting married. Mrs Jones told me _____.
5 They have no right to take any credit for the success of the project, we did it all _____.
6 You must answer the questions _____. I'm not going to help any of you.
7 She broke it _____ and then tried to blame me.
8 It was a terrible play. The actors _____ didn't understand it.

15 **on one's own, by oneself**

Look at these sentences:

She doesn't like being left **on her own** in the evenings. She gets nervous.

She doesn't like being left **by herself** in the evenings. She gets nervous.
I didn't give the children any help with the project. They did it **on their own**.
I didn't give the children any help with the project. They did it **by themselves**.

The forms of **on one's own, by oneself** can be used to suggest either the idea of being alone or of doing something without help. They have the same meaning, so **on my own** means the same as **by myself** and so on.

Complete each of the following sentences in two ways using the correct form of **on one's own** or **by oneself**:

1 *A* Did you help Jimmy to make that model aeroplane?
   B No, he did it _____.
2 They didn't need to ask anyone the way. They found the house _____.
3 I don't know how you can stand living in the country _____. I'd get bored if I were you.
4 I'm very independent so I like to work _____.
5 We designed this house _____. We didn't have an architect to help us.
6 She learnt to play the piano _____, without a teacher.

16 **what, the thing that**

a **what is interesting, the interesting thing**
Compare these sentences:

What is interesting about this is that it was proved by two different methods.
The interesting thing about this is that it was proved by two different methods.

Change one form to the other in these sentences:

1 The surprising thing is that it took them so long to find out.
2 What is exciting about it is that it's never happened before.
3 What is unfortunate is that we didn't realise the mistake until it was too late.
4 The depressing thing in Britain is the weather.

b **what interests me, the thing that interests me**
Compare these sentences:

What interests me in their research is the method they used.
The thing that interests me in their research is the method they used.

Change one form to the other in these sentences:

1 The thing that worries me is my father's reaction.
2 What pleases me about it is that the problem was solved without any arguments.
3 The thing that matters most is your own health.
4 What annoys me is that they are so rude.

c what I like, the thing I like

Compare these sentences:

What I like about it is the simplicity of the design.
The thing I like about it is the simplicity of the design.

Change one form to the other in these sentences:

1 The thing I hate about Monday mornings is having to go back to work.
2 What I disapprove of is their lack of consideration for other people.
3 The thing I complain about is their selfishness.
4 The thing I can't understand is how they made the mistake in the first place.

d what and that

Compare these sentences:

What interests him is money.
What he cares about is money.
The only **thing that** interests him is money.
Money is **the** only **thing (that)** he cares about.

Use **what** or **that** in each space in the following dialogue:

Harvey, a theatre director in a small provincial town, is talking to Judy, an actress.

Judy   The play went quite well. The only thing __1__ bothered me was the size of the audience. And the only part of the play __2__ interested them was the end.

Harvey   __3__ you must understand is that people in this town don't come to the theatre to think. The only thing __4__ keeps their attention is something exciting. __5__ they like is a good story. The play __6__ has drawn the biggest audience this year was a murder mystery.

Judy   That's __7__ upsets me. And __8__ I learnt at drama school doesn't help me. When I got this job I thought it was the best thing __9__ had ever happened to me, but now the only thought __10__ comes into my head on the stage is: When will it be over? That's __11__ depresses me so much.

Harvey   __12__   is worrying me is that if we don't get a bigger audience we'll have to close the theatre. The only solution __13__ occurs to me is to give them __14__ they want. It's a pity but __15__ draws the crowds in London isn't popular here.

17 Adjectives, pronouns, **belong to** and genitive

a **my, mine, belongs to me**
Compare the forms in these sentences:

It isn't **my book**. The book isn't **mine**. The book **doesn't belong to me**.
It's **his car**. The car's **his**. The car **belongs to him**.
Whose shoes are these? **Whose** are these shoes? **Who do** these shoes **belong to**?

Rewrite each of these sentences twice, using the two other alternatives, as in the examples above:

1 It isn't my money.
2 The house is theirs.
3 I think this pen belongs to you.
4 It's her camera.
5 Those horses aren't his.
6 Whose is this newspaper?
7 The dog's ours.
8 The racquet doesn't belong to me.
9 Hey! That's my suitcase.
10 Whose stockings are these?

b Genitive and **belong to**
Compare the forms in these sentences:

The table was **King Edward's**. It wasn't **King Arthur's**.
It was **King Edward's table**. It wasn't **King Arthur's**. (table)
The table **belonged to King Edward**. It **didn't belong to King Arthur**.

Rewrite these sentences, using the alternative forms, as in the examples above:

1 That car is Fred's.
2 That house over there is my sister's.
3 The factory isn't her father's. It's her uncle's.
4 It's my cousin's farm. It's not my brother's.
5 That's Jack Smith's car, isn't it?
6 It was my grandfather's watch.
7 The castle was the duke's at one time, wasn't it?
8 When he dies, it will be his son's land.

18 **one of my friends, a friend of mine**

Compare these sentences:

One of my friends works there.
A friend of mine works there.

Rewrite these sentences, using the alternative form, as in the examples above:

1 She's getting married to one of my cousins.
2 A friend of hers gave me a lift home.
3 I used to go out with one of his colleagues.
4 I thought he was one of your relations.
5 I bought it from one of their business acquaintances.
6 Giving each other presents at New Year is one of our family customs.
7 Isn't he an employee of yours?
8 I lent him an old tennis racquet of mine.
9 He's offered me a job in one of his companies.
10 One of my uncles has just died.

19 Genitive

a Punctuation

Look at the punctuation of these sentences:

The **artist's** pictures were so good that they were all sold.
The **artists'** pictures were so good that they were all sold.

In the first case, there was only one artist; in the second, more than one.

Note that **the picture of the artist** refers to a picture painted by another person where the artist was the subject. Similarly, **the pictures of the artists** refers to pictures painted by other people where the artists were the subjects.

When a noun has an irregular plural, not ending in s, the apostrophe comes before the s, e.g. **men's, women's, children's, people's.**

In these sentences the words in brackets should end in **s'** if plural or **'s** if singular. Write out these words in the correct form:

Charles and Molly have four children, Edward and Henry, aged 18, who are twins, Carol, 17, and Mary, 16.

1 Edward and Henry played together in the school tennis championship and won the doubles. Their parents saw the (boy) victory.
2 Molly says: The (twin) clothes are no problem. Edward can always wear his (brother) clothes and vice versa. But I spend a lot of money on the (girl) clothes. They always want to look different.
3 The twins are in the same class but the girls are in different classes. Charles says to the (twin) teacher: I'm worried about my (son) exam results. They've both done badly. He says to (Carol) teacher: What can you tell me about my (daughter) progress? Her results were not as good as her (sister).

4 Henry says: I don't agree with all my (parent) ideas. For instance, my (father) views on politics are very right-wing, and my (mother) attitude towards my (sister) boy-friends is sometimes a bit intolerant. Still, they're both more reasonable than some of my (friend) parents.

b Genitive with expressions of time
Compare the following sentences, studying the punctuation:

I'll see you in **a week's time**.
I'll see you in **three weeks' time**.

Note that **a fortnight's time** is two weeks' time.
The genitive, with **'s**, is used for people, animals and periods of time, but not for things, except in a few phrases.

In these sentences the words in brackets should end in s' if plural or 's if singular. Write out these words in the correct form:

1 I'm going away for a (fortnight) holiday.
2 He gets a (month) holiday every year.
3 The doctor says he needs a few (week) rest.
4 This (year) students are better than last (year).
5 The town will be completely different in a few (year) time.
6 I couldn't get (today) newspaper, so I've brought (yesterday).
7 In six (month) time, he is going to retire, and after forty (year) work in the same firm, he deserves a gold watch.
8 In a few (minute) time, the race will begin.

c Genitive and the use of **one(s)**
Compare these sentences:

I like this car better than **the American one**.	(the car made in America)
I like this car better than **the American's**.	(the car which belongs to the American)
I like this car better than **the Americans'**.	(the car which belongs to the Americans)

Note that we do not use **one(s)** after a genitive.

Complete these sentences by adding **one(s)**, **'s** or **s'**:

1 These ties are not as smart as the Italian _____ we bought last week.
2 Our yacht was not as fast as the Norwegian _____. They had a better crew.
3 Indian elephants are much easier to train than African _____.
4 I think our chances of winning are better than the German _____. Our team is very experienced.
5 Borg and McEnroe are both good players but the Swede _____. behaviour on court is better than the American _____.

d the grocer's

Look at this sentence:

Susan, would you go to **the grocer's** and get me some flour.

The grocer's means 'the grocer's shop'. Shops are sometimes referred to as **the grocer's, the baker's, the butcher's**, when we do not use the actual name of the shop.

Where, in Britain, would you expect to buy: meat, bread, vegetables, fish, cigarettes, medicine, flowers, nails, sugar, newspapers?

Adjectives

20   Comparatives and superlatives
a   One-syllable and three-syllable adjectives
Notice the forms of the adjectives in these sentences:

He's **taller** than his sister; in fact, he's **the tallest** in the family.
But she's **more intelligent** than he is. She's **the most intelligent** person I've ever met.

One-syllable adjectives form the comparative with **-er** and the superlative with **-est**; adjectives with three syllables or more form the comparative with **more** and the superlative with **most**.
Note the irregular forms: **good, better, best; bad, worse, worst**.

Complete the sentences with the correct form of the adjectives given in brackets:

1   He's _____ than his sister. She's the _____ of the family, in fact. (old, young)
2   It's the _____ victory of his career. Now everyone agrees that he's the _____ player in the world. (important, good)
3   It's a _____ car than the previous model but I think the other one was _____. (fast, reliable)
4   He's been elected the _____ actor in the country but I think he's the _____ actor I've ever seen. (popular, bad)
5   The new machine is _____ than the old one and also _____. It costs less but washes clothes better. (cheap, efficient)

b   Two-syllable adjectives
Notice the forms of the adjectives in these sentences:

That house is **prettier** than the last one we looked at; in fact, I think it's **the prettiest** we've seen so far.
Cathy is **more cheerful** than her sister; actually she's **the most cheerful** person I know.

Two-syllable adjectives usually form the comparative with **more** and the superlative with **most**. But an important group (those ending in **-y**, e.g. **happy, easy, lucky**) form the comparative with **-er** and the superlative with **-est**. Note that the **-y** changes to i, e.g. **happier, happiest**.
Other groups taking **-er** and **-est** are those ending in **-le** (**noble, gentle**), **-ow** (**narrow, yellow**) and **-er** (**clever, tender**).
All others, e.g. those ending in **-ful**, **-less** (**cheerful, useless**), usually take **more** and **most**.
In a few cases, e.g. **common, stupid, unfair, unkind, pleasant**, both the **-er/-est** and **more/most** forms are found.

Complete the sentences with the correct form of the adjectives given in brackets:

1 He's one of the _____ people in the town but he's also one of the _____. He never stops working. (wealthy, active)

2 The _____ streets in the town are also the _____ because there is so much traffic. (narrow, noisy)

3 She was the kindest, _____ person I've ever known. Even when she was ill, she was _____ than most of us are when we are well. (gentle, cheerful)

4 He's the _____ assistant I've ever had. And the _____! Jones was _____ than he is and _____ but the only time you ever see Smith work is at meals. He's the _____ fellow I've ever seen. (useless, stupid, careless, lazy, greedy)

5 People say I'm _____ than he is, but that's not true. I get better results because I'm _____. (clever, thorough)

21 Making comparisons

Look at these sentences:

> A Dalmatian is **more intelligent than** a Scottish terrier but **less easy** to train. It is not **as brave as** a Doberman.

This information comes from the table opposite, which shows how different breeds of dog vary in their temperament and also in their height and weight. A + sign in the category **intelligent** means that a certain breed is very intelligent. A 0 sign means that a certain breed is of average intelligence. A − sign means that a certain breed is not intelligent.

Use information given in the table on p. 29 to complete the exercises below.

a **-er than, more . . . than**

> The Belgian sheepdog is **easier to train than** the Boxer.
> The Belgian sheepdog is **more intelligent than** the English sheepdog.

1 Make five comparisons, using **gentler, livelier, calmer, stronger** and **braver**, as in the first example above.

2 Make four comparisons, using **more aggressive, more intelligent, more suspicious towards strangers**, and **more faithful**, as in the second example above.

b **as (so) . . . as**

> The Chow-chow is not **as (so) fond of children as** the Scottish terrier.
> The Belgian sheepdog is **as tall as** the English sheepdog.
> The Chow-chow is **about as heavy as** the Pyrenean sheepdog.

Temperament and size	Sheepdogs			Guard Dogs			House Dogs			
	Belgian sheepdog	Pyrenean sheepdog	English sheepdog	Boxer	Doberman	Rottweiler	Cairn Terrier	Scottish Terrier	Dalmatian	Chow-chow
Intelligent	+	0	0	0	+	+	0	0	+	0
Gentle	−	0	0	−	−	+	0	0	0	0
Lively	0	+	−	0	+	−	+	+	+	−
Easy to train	+	0	+	−	0	+	+	−	−	0
Fond of children	0	0	+	+	0	0	+	+	0	0
Suspicious of strangers	+	+	−	0	+	0	−	0	0	+
Faithful	+	+	0	+	+	0	0	+	+	+
Strong	0	+	+	+	+	+	0	+	+	+
Brave	+	+	0	+	+	0	0	+	0	0
Height (cm.)	60	50	60	62	69	64	28	27	58	50
Weight (kg.)	28	22	60	30	35	50	7	10	24	21

+ = above average
0 = average
− = below average

If one breed is **gentler** than another, we can say it is **less aggressive.**
If it is **not as lively,** we can say it is **calmer.**
If it is **more suspicious** of strangers, we can say it is **not as friendly.**

1 Make comparisons using **as (so) . . . as** with all the other adjectives in the table, as in the first example above.

2 Make comparisons using **as tall as**, **as heavy as**, **about as tall as**, **about as heavy as**, as in the second and third examples above.

c **the same . . . as**

> The Belgian sheepdog is **about the same height as** the English sheepdog.
> The Chow-chow **weighs about as much as** the Pyrenean sheepdog.

1 Rewrite the answers you wrote in Section b with **as tall as** and **about as tall as**, using **the same height as** and **about the same height as**, as in the first example above.

2 Rewrite the answers you wrote in Section b with **as heavy as** and **about as heavy as**, using **weighs about as much as**, as in the second example above.

d **much/a lot -er, much/a lot more . . .**

> The English sheepdog is **much (a lot) heavier** than the Cairn terrier.

1 Make comparisons, using **much more aggressive, much livelier, much calmer, much easier to train, much friendlier, much more suspicious of strangers, much heavier, much taller, much bigger, much smaller**. You can use **a lot** instead of **much**.

e **the -est, the most . . ., the least . . .**

> The English sheepdog is **the calmest**. (of the three breeds of sheepdog)
> The Boxer is **the least intelligent**. (of the three breeds of guard dog)
> The Chow-chow is **the least lively**. (of the four breeds of house dog)

1 Make comparisons between the different breeds of sheepdog, using **most aggressive, liveliest, calmest, friendliest, least faithful, shortest, heaviest, lightest**, as in the first example above.

2 Compare the different guard dogs, using **least intelligent, gentlest, liveliest, calmest, easiest to train, most difficult to train, most suspicious of strangers, tallest, shortest, heaviest, lightest,** as in the second example above.

3 Make comparisons between the different house dogs, using **most intelligent, calmest, friendliest, most suspicious of strangers, least faithful, bravest, heaviest, lightest, tallest, shortest**, as in the third example above.

22 Exclamations: **How exciting! What an exciting day!**

Compare the forms used in these sentences:

How exciting! How tall he is! **How lovely** it is!
What nonsense! **What** awful weather!
What a pity! **What a** pretty girl!
What manners! **What** beautiful eyes! (she has)

In the exercises below, imagine you are in the position of the people mentioned. Think of some of the exclamations they might make:

a *Jean is on holiday at the seaside.*
   e.g.   The hotel is very comfortable.
        What a comfortable hotel!
        How comfortable it is!

1 Her room is very pleasant.
2 The weather is marvellous.
3 She has a beautiful view.
4 The beach is very long.
5 The air is warm.
6 The water is very blue.
7 Some children are playing on the beach; she thinks they are sweet.
8 They are very happy.
9 There are some beautiful yachts in the harbour.
10 In the restaurant, everything is very clean.
11 The service is very good.
12 The food is tasty.
13 The people at her table are friendly.
14 The manager is very polite.
15 He tells her about a coach trip which she thinks will be very interesting.
16 The tickets are too expensive; it is a pity she can't afford it.

b *Pamela is at the cinema with her boy-friend.*
1 They are watching a very romantic film.
2 The hero is tall, strong and handsome.
3 He has blue eyes and fair hair.
4 There is romantic music in the background.
5 It is a sad scene.
6 The heroine is saying goodbye to the hero for ever; it is very moving.
7 Jim thinks the film is rubbish.
8 He thinks the hero is an idiot.
9 The heroine is very pretty.
10 But the story is absurd.
11 The acting is terrible.
12 He thinks it was a waste of money to go to the cinema.

23 so, such, such a/an

Compare the forms used in these sentences:

The weather was so awful! We had **such** awful weather. (mass noun)
She's **so** pretty! She's **such a** pretty girl! (singular noun)
His manners are **so** appalling. He has **such** appalling manners.
(plural noun)

Notice that we use **so** + adjective, **such** + mass noun or plural noun
and **such a** + singular noun.

Complete the exercises below, using **so**, **such** or **such a**:

a I had __1__ wonderful holiday. The hotel was __2__
comfortable. My room was __3__ pleasant and I had __4__ a
beautiful view. The beach was __5__ long, the air was __6__
warm and the water was __7__ blue. I've never seen __8__ clear
water. The service in the restaurant was __9__ good, too, and I've
never had __10__ good food. I met __11__ friendly people, too,
and the manager was __12__ polite. He had __13__ good ideas
about trips around the island, but they were __14__ expensive that I
couldn't afford to go on many of them. It was __15__ pity.

b It was __1__ lovely film. It was __2__ romantic. And Robert
Redford is __3__ handsome. He has __4__ blue eyes and
__5__ magnificent fair hair. But the scenes were __6__ sad and
they played __7__ romantic music. I couldn't help crying. There
was __8__ sad scene when the girl said goodbye to him.

c I've never seen __1__ rubbish. It was __2__ boring. It was
__3__ stupid story and the acting was __4__ terrible that I would
have walked out if I hadn't been with Pamela. They say Robert
Redford's __5__ good-looking fellow and __6__ marvellous actor
but I suppose no one can act with __7__ awful dialogue.

24 so, such, so much, such a lot of

a so ... that, such (a/an) ... that

Compare these sentences:

The organisation is **so big that** it employs a million people.
It's **such a big organisation that** it employs a million people.

The students are **so intelligent that** they hardly need a teacher.
They're **such intelligent students that** they hardly need a teacher.

This bread is **so good that** I could eat it all day.
It's **such good bread that** I could eat it all day.

Rewrite these sentences, using the alternative form, as in the examples above:

1 He's such a tall man that he has to have all his clothes specially
made.

2 The film was so successful that it ran for two years.
3 The music was so beautiful that I listened to it for hours.
4 The secretaries are so efficient that they could get a job anywhere.
5 She had to go to bed because her headache was so bad.
6 He plays so well that a professional team has offered him a contract.
7 He was such a kind man that she trusted him completely.
8 The weather was so good that we lay on the beach all day.
9 It was such a long journey that they felt tired at the end of it.
10 The owner and his wife were such pleasant people that we've decided to stay there again next year.

b **so much, such a lot of**

Compare these sentences:

He spent **so much** money on his house that he went bankrupt.
He spent **such a lot of** money on his house that he went bankrupt.

He bought **so many** apples that we'll be eating them for weeks.
He bought **such a lot of** apples that we'll be eating them for weeks.

Rewrite these sentences, using the alternative form, as in the examples above:
1 I don't like coal fires. They make so much smoke.
2 She eats such a lot of bread that it has made her fat.
3 I don't know why you need so many clothes.
4 He earns so much money that he doesn't know what to spend it on.
5 This road's very dangerous. There have been such a lot of accidents here.
6 I can't come out this evening. I've got such a lot of work to do.

25 **so ... that, too ... for**

Compare these sentences:

He was **so** far out **that** no one could reach him.
He was **too** far out **for anyone to reach** him.

The court was **so** wet **that** we couldn't play tennis.
The court was **too** wet **for us to play** tennis.

Rewrite these sentences, using the alternative form, as in the examples above:
1 The accident was so serious that I'll never forget it.
2 The book was too interesting for me to put down.
3 The street is so narrow that cars cannot pass one another.
4 The weather was so bad that they couldn't go climbing.
5 He's too ill for anyone to visit him.
6 The questions were too difficult for me to answer.

26 be used to

Look at these sentences:

I'm **used to** children. I have seven of them myself.
I'm **used to** getting up early. I've been doing it for years.
I'm **not used to** flying. I usually go by sea.
He **wasn't used to** washing his own clothes. His mother had always done it for him.

Note that **be used to** is always followed by a gerund (**-ing**) or a noun. It can be used with any tense of the verb **be**. **Used** means 'accustomed'; it indicates a habit formed by experience.

Look at the example and answer the interviewer's questions in the same way, with **be used to**:
Bill Collins has applied for a job as a bus driver.

e.g. ***Mr Batt***	Now, in this job, you'll have to get up early.
Bill	**That's all right. I'm used to getting up early. (I've been doing it for years.)**
Mr Batt	You'll have to drive heavy vehicles.
Bill	_____.
Mr Batt	You'll have to work in bad weather.
Bill	_____.
Mr Batt	You'll have to do overtime when necessary.
Bill	_____.
Mr Batt	You'll have to work at weekends.
Bill	_____.
Mr Batt	You'll have to travel a lot.
Bill	_____.
Mr Batt	You'll have to deal with difficult people.
Bill	_____.
Mr Batt	You'll have to be patient when people are rude to you.
Bill	_____.
Mr Batt	Above all, you'll have to do what you're told.
Bill	_____.
Mr Batt	Good heavens! What a reasonable man! What have you been doing all these years?
Bill	I've been in the army. I was a lorry driver.

27 Comparison of adverbs (irregular forms)

Look at these sentences:

    A Why didn't you run **faster**?
    B I ran **as fast as** I could.
    A Why didn't you work **harder**?
    B I worked **as hard as** I could.

a **fast** and **hard**

Complete these sentences in the same way with the correct forms of **fast** and **hard**:

1 *A* If you worked _____ I'd pay you more money.
    B I work as _____ as the others do. In fact, I work _____ than some of them.
2 *A* I can run _____ than my brother, and he's older than me.
    B If you can run _____ why didn't you beat him in the race yesterday?
    A I fell down, and when I got up I ran as _____ as I could, but I couldn't catch him.

b **better/worse than, as well/badly as**

Look at these sentences:

The children behaved **as well as** can be expected.
You're behaving **as badly as** your brother.

The horse runs **better** when the ground is soft.
It doesn't run **as (so) well** when the ground is hard.

Most people treat snakes **worse than** rats.
Most people don't treat rats **as (so) badly as** snakes.

Complete these sentences in the same way, using **as well (as), as badly (as), better** or **worse**:

1 Jack didn't play _____ usual today. I thought he'd beat Harry. Harry deserved to win, though. He certainly played _____ than Jack.
2 I've never known a boss who treated his staff _____ he does. He treats them _____ than animals.
3 The army fought _____ could be expected in those difficult conditions. I don't think any soldiers in the world would have fought _____.
4 My father drives _____ than anyone I know. He's had three accidents already this year. Even my mother doesn't drive _____ he does, and she's so bad that I won't travel with her.

NOTE For the difference between **hard** and **hardly**, see Practice 30.

28 **the more . . . the more**

Look at these sentences:

> **The more** he works, **the more tired** he gets.
> **The bigger** the car, **the more expensive** it is to run.
> **The less** you argue, **the better** it will be for you.

Note the form: **the** + comparative . . . **the** + comparative

Put the adjectives and adverbs in brackets into the comparative form to complete these sentences, as in the examples above:

1 The _____ students, the _____ it is to teach them. The _____
   they are, the _____ they understand. (good, easy, intelligent, soon)
2 The _____ you eat, the _____ you get, and the _____ you get,
   the _____ you are to have a heart attack. (much, fat, fat, likely)
3 The _____ the whisky is matured, the _____ it tastes, but, on the
   other hand, the _____ the care needed to mature it, the _____ it
   is. (long, good, great, expensive)
4 The _____ he gets, the _____ he becomes. He's got a bad back
   and the trouble is that the _____ exercise he gets, the _____ it
   becomes. (old, irritable, little, bad)
5 The _____ I think about it, the _____ I understand why he
   behaved like that. I sometimes think that the _____ you treat
   people, the _____ they respond to you and the _____ they are.
   (much, little, good, bad, ungrateful)

29 **quite, rather**

Compare these sentences:

> I think London's **quite** an attractive city.
> Do you? I think it's **rather** dirty and noisy.

In general, we use **quite** to mean 'comparatively' when we are in favour
of something and **rather** when we are more critical of it. Most people
think it is a good thing to be tall, so we usually say,
e.g. **She's quite tall.**
      She's rather short.
But in some circumstances, this may not be true,
e.g. **She's rather tall to be a ballet dancer.** (because most dancers are
      not tall and she may find it difficult to get a partner of her height)
With the comparative form of the adjectives, we can only use **rather**. In
this case, it doesn't matter whether we think something is good or bad,
e.g. *A* **How's your mother?**
      B **She's been ill, but fortunately she's rather better today.**

Complete these sentences with **quite** or **rather**:

1 Most of the book is _____ dull, but the end is _____ interesting.
2 The first question was _____ easy but the rest were _____ difficult.
3 *A* That's _____ expensive. Haven't you got anything cheaper?
   B This one's _____ cheap, only £5.
   A Oh, yes, that's _____ more reasonable.
4 She was _____ plain when she was young, but she's improved with the years, and now I find her _____ more attractive.
5 *A* The house is _____ pleasant but we're looking for something _____ larger. We have six children, you see.
   B Ah, you have _____ a large family.
   A Yes, so it's _____ difficult to find the right kind of accommodation.
   B Well, we have some _____ new chalets on the other side of the bay. They might be _____ more suitable. You would have to take two chalets but they're _____ near so they would be _____ convenient for meals and so on.

30 **hard/hardly**

Compare these sentences:

> She works very **hard**.
> He had such a strange accent that I could **hardly** understand him.
> He **hardly** ate anything for breakfast this morning. (He ate almost nothing.)

Hardly means 'almost not' or 'almost no'.
With an adjective, e.g. **hardly surprising**, **hardly** means 'not very';
hardly ever means 'almost never',
e.g. *A* **Rovers lost on Saturday.**
      B **That's hardly surprising. After all, they hardly ever win.**

Complete these sentences with **hard**, **hardly** or **hardly ever**:

1 You shouldn't work so _____. You'll have a heart attack.
2 I'll just have a cup of coffee, thanks. I _____ eat anything in the morning, except on Sundays, when I get up late.
3 I got to the station so late that I _____ had time to buy a ticket and catch the train.
4 You'll pass the examination if you try _____.
5 It's _____ surprising that he failed. He did _____ any work.
6 He _____ does any work. I've only seen him look at a book once or twice since the beginning of term.
7 Is anything wrong with the wine? You've _____ touched it.
8 The British usually drink tea or wine with their meals. They _____ drink champagne except on special occasions.

31 ever, never

Compare these sentences:

I've **never** seen such a beautiful house.
It's the most beautiful house I've **ever** seen.

They've **never** drunk **so much** wine in Britain.
They've drunk **more** wine in Britain this year **than ever**.
They're drinking **more** wine **than ever** in Britain.

She has **never** played **so well**. (before)
She is playing **better than ever**.

Rewrite these sentences, using the alternative form with **ever** or **never**, as in the examples above:

1   I've never heard such a ridiculous story.
2   He's working harder than ever.
3   The weather has never been so bad as it has been this year.
4   Prices are rising faster than ever.
5   The country has never consumed so much oil.

32 still, yet, already

Notice the use of **still, yet** and **already** in these sentences:

    A   Has the Post Office opened **yet**?
    B   No, it's only five to nine.

Why is the butcher's **still** open? It's half past six.

    A   When does the garage open?
    B   It's **already** open. It opens at eight.

Look at the passage and table of information below. You will need to use the information from the table to do the exercise at the end.

The workers at the ABC factory are supposed to start work at 8.00 in the morning and finish at 5.00 in the evening. The manager wants to know if they arrive late and leave early. He speaks to the foreman at 8.05 in the morning and at 5.05 in the afternoon.

Name	Arrived	Left
Adams	7.55	5.00
Baker	8.10	5.10
Chase	8.00	5.03
Day	8.20	5.15
Evans	7.50	5.20
Fox	8.30	4.35

At 8.05 in the morning

Manager Has Adams arrived yet?

Foreman Yes, he's already here. He arrived ten minutes ago.

Manager Has Baker arrived yet?

Foreman No, he hasn't arrived yet.

At 5.05 in the afternoon

Manager Is Adams still here?

Foreman No, he's already gone home. He left five minutes ago.

Manager Is Baker still here?

Foreman Yes, he's still in the factory. He hasn't gone home yet.

Ask and answer questions in the same way about the other workers for the morning and afternoon.

33 no longer, not . . . any more

Compare the answers to the questions:

A Does John Pratt still live here?

B No, he doesn't live here **any more**.

No, he **no longer** lives here.

No longer is more formal than **not . . . any more** and is not used so much in spoken English.

Rewrite these sentences, using the alternative form, as in the examples above:

1 He no longer loves her.
2 They no longer work there.
3 At one time there was a great deal of unemployment in this area but that is not true any more.
4 The Ministry does not require motorists to renew their licences every five years any more.
5 I no longer feel lonely.

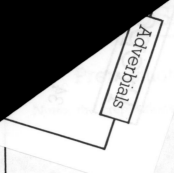

: in, out, on, off, into, out of, on to

in these sentences:
Look, there's a boat **on** the lake. (floating on the surface)
He's **in** the water. (swimming)
He took his hat **off**. (it was on his head)
The dentist took my tooth **out**. (it was in my head)
He got **into** the car. He got **on to** his bicycle.
He fell **out of** his pram. He fell **off** the roof.

In almost always suggests 'inside' in English; **on** means 'on the surface of'.
Out is the opposite of **in**, and **off** is the opposite of **on**.
With verbs of movement, when there is an object, we use **into** and **out of**, **on to** and **off**.
We say **get on** and **get off** for a bus and **get in** and **get out of** for a train,

e.g.   **You must get out at the next station.** (train)
          You must get off at the next stop. (bus)

This is because buses did not have closing doors until recently in Britain.
We would normally use **get out of** for a coach, because coaches have always had doors.

Complete the following sentences with **in, on, out, off, into, on to** or **out of**:

1   The bread is _____ the table _____ the kitchen.
2   He lives _____ that house, _____ the second floor.
3   I'm not going to buy this shirt. There is a hole _____ it and there are some dirty marks _____ the sleeve.
4   He stayed at a little village _____ the mountains.
5   There aren't any houses _____ Mount Everest.
6   Sit _____ that chair and keep quiet!
7   Would you like to sit _____ this armchair?
8   *A*   Is Johnny at home?
     B   No, he's gone _____.
9   We had a puncture so we had to take the tyre _____ and put another one _____.
10   I can't speak properly because I've taken my false teeth _____.
       Wait till I put them _____ again.
11   Johnny went _____ half an hour ago. He'll be back soon.
12   Johnny went _____ the house half an hour ago.
13   He sat proudly _____ his horse.
14   I must go to the bank to get my money.
       I must get my money _____ the bank before it closes.

35 home, at home

Compare these sentences:

> A Is Mr Jones **in**? (the house)
> B No, I'm afraid he's **out**.
> A Is Mr Jones **at home**?
> B No, I'm afraid he's **not at home**.

At is the only preposition used with **home**.
No preposition is used with verbs of movement,

e.g.   A **What time did he arrive home?**
       (What time did he arrive at his house?)
    B **He got home at ten o'clock.**
       (He got to his house at ten o'clock.)

Complete the sentences with the appropriate preposition, when one is required:

1 If I stayed _____ home all day, like you, I'd be bored.
2 When you invite people _____ the house, you must be polite.
3 When you invite people _____ home, you must be polite.
4 Come _____ home with me.
5 The President drove back _____ the White House.
6 I called _____ his house and knocked at the door but there was no one _____ home.
7 When I arrived _____ home, my son and daughter were both _____.

36 Prepositions of time

Study this list of prepositions before completing the exercise:

at:
exact points of time, **at 5 o'clock, at dinner time, at this moment**, festivals, **at Christmas, at Easter, at New Year**
at night, (but **during the day**), **at weekends, at the weekend**

on:
days and dates, **on Monday, on June 10th, on Christmas Day, on a summer evening, on a Sunday morning, on Wednesday night**

in:
longer periods of time, **in August, in spring, in 1968, in the twentieth century, in the Middle Ages, in the past, in the future**
periods of time within which or at the end of which something may happen, **in five minutes, in three years' time**
in the morning, in the afternoon, in the evening

by:
By means 'at some time not later than'.
I'll pay you at the end of the month. (on the 30th or 31st)

I'll pay you by the end of the month. (at some time before the end but certainly not later than the 30th or 31st)

Complete the sentences with the correct prepositions:

1   We never go out _____ Sundays.
2   It's usually quiet here _____ Sunday mornings.
3   He got up early _____ the morning although he knew he would not go to bed until late _____ night.
4   I always play tennis _____ the weekend.
5   The leaves fall from the trees _____ autumn.
6   It snows a lot here _____ winter.
7   He has a long holiday _____ the summer and shorter holidays _____ Christmas and Easter.
8   The concert will begin _____ 7.30.
9   I'll see you _____ lunchtime.
10 Dinner will be ready _____ a few minutes.
11 It's nice to have the family around you _____ Christmas.
12 We're having a party _____ Christmas Day.
13 She got up early _____ Christmas morning.
14 He was born _____ June 1st.
15 He was born _____ 1956.
16 He died _____ the nineteenth century.
17 He's old-fashioned. He's still living _____ the past.
18 She was born _____ 1.30 _____ the morning _____ April 3rd, 1953.
19 *A* The programme starts _____ half an hour's time.
    B Don't worry. I won't be long. I'll be back _____ then.
20 It's very warm here _____ the day but it's cold _____ night.

NOTE   For **since**, **for**, **from** and **to**, see Practice 122.

37   **made of/from/with/by**

Notice the preposition used in each sentence:

The table is **made of** wood. (It is still recognisably wood.)
Wine is **made from** grapes. (We cannot see the grapes in the wine.)
The cake was **made with** flour, butter, eggs, sugar and fruit. (a number of different ingredients)
The furniture was **made by** my grandfather. (My grandfather made it.)

Supply the correct preposition in each sentence:

1   Knives are made _____ stainless steel.
2   Whisky is made _____ barley or rye.
3   The model boats are made _____ retired sailors.
4   Trifle is a dessert made _____ cake, custard, fruit and cream.

5   The dial on the telephone is made _____ plastic.
6   Artificial silk is a fibre made _____ a kind of plastic.
7   The wastepaper basket was made _____ Plastics Limited.
8   Paper is made _____ trees.
9   What's it made _____? Gold, or platinum?
10 *A* What have you put in it?
    B I made it _____ red wine, lemonade, a little brandy and some gin.

38   **without**

a   without + noun

Compare these sentences:

He went out. He didn't take his umbrella.
He went out **without his umbrella**.

Rewrite these sentences, using **without** followed by a noun:

e.g.   This contract is worthless until he signs it.
       This contract is worthless **without his signature**.
1   When you go out, don't leave your hat behind.
    Don't go out _____.
2   I can't pay the cheque unless you sign it.
    I can't pay the cheque _____.
3   I can do it by myself. I don't need your help.
    I can do it by myself _____.
4   He completed the test and there wasn't a single mistake.
    He completed the test _____.
5   Oh, dear! I've come out and haven't got any money.
    Oh, dear! I've come out _____.

b   without + gerund

Compare these sentences:

He went out. He didn't say anything.
He went out **without saying** anything.

Rewrite these sentences, using **without** followed by a verb in the gerund form:

e.g.   Say goodbye before you go.
       Don't go **without saying goodbye**.
1   How can you earn a living, if you don't work?
    How can you earn a living _____.
2   It's silly to go sailing if you don't take the proper equipment.
    It's silly to go sailing _____.
3   He left the restaurant. He hadn't paid the bill.
    He left the restaurant _____.
4   He always exaggerates when he tells a story.
    He can't tell a story _____.

5   I laugh every time I read that book.
    I can't read that book _____ .

39   until, as far as

Notice the use of **until** and **as far as** in these sentences:

I won't be able to finish it **until** the end of the month.
Go **as far as** the station and then turn right.

Until relates to time, **as far as** to distance.

Use **until** or **as far as** to complete the following sentences:
1   The restaurant does not open _____ seven o'clock.
2   We went _____ the castle, but then we felt tired and turned back.
3   We walked _____ we got tired. Then we sat down and had a rest.
4   I don't think you'll get _____ the village before it gets dark.
5   We played tennis _____ it got dark.
6   We could see _____ the sea from the top of the mountain.

40   because, because of, due to

Compare these sentences:

He couldn't come **because** he was ill.
He couldn't come **because of** his illness.
His absence was **due to** his illness. (his being ill)

Because is followed by a subject and verb. **Because of** and **due to** are complex prepositions (two-word prepositions) and are followed by a noun.

Rewrite each of the following sentences in two different ways, using **because**, **because of** and **due to**:
1   English people probably drink more wine now because of their memories of holidays by the Mediterranean.
    a   English people probably drink more wine now because they _____ .
    b   The increase in wine drinking in England is probably _____ .
2   He has psychological problems because he was unhappy as a child.
    a   He has psychological problems because of his _____ .
    b   His psychological problems are _____ .
3   We have increased our prices because of the rise in the cost of living.
    a   We have increased our prices because the _____ .
    b   The increases in our prices are _____ .

4 The changes in the programme are due to the poor quality of pictures received from the Himalayas.
  a We have made changes in the programme because of _____.
  b We have made changes in the programme because we _____.

5 The performance has been cancelled because the leading actor is ill.
  a The performance has been cancelled because _____.
  b The cancellation of the performance is _____.

6 The firm's poor performance this year is due to our failure to obtain new customers.
  a The firm has performed badly this year because of _____.
  b The firm has performed badly this year because we _____.

41 as, like

a **as** and **like** to describe the way in which actions are done
Compare these sentences:

> Do **as** I say.
> Do it **like** this.
> He's been very ill. He walks and talks **like** an old man.
> **As** I said last week, we must do something about the rubbish in our streets.

We use **as** + clause (subject and verb) and **like** + noun, pronoun or adverb.

Complete these sentences with **as** or **like**:

1 A I can't understand why he behaved _____ that.
  B Well, you never know if people are going to behave _____ you expect them to.

2 You should pay attention to the teacher, _____ me.

3 You should pay attention to the teacher, _____ the rest of us do.

4 _____ I was saying, he stays in bed all morning, just _____ his father. If I'd known he was going to grow up _____ that, I wouldn't have let him do _____ he liked when he was younger. _____ you know, I've always been soft with him because he's the youngest. I should have brought him up _____ his brothers and sisters.

b **as a referee, like a monkey**
Compare these sentences:

> He works **as a referee** on Saturday afternoons. (It is his job; he really is a referee.)
> He can climb **like a monkey**. (but he isn't a monkey)

We use **to work as** or **to have a job as** to talk about someone's actual job, profession or social position.
When we say X is **like** something or someone, we mean that X is similar to that thing or that person.

Complete these sentences with **as** or **like**:

1 I worked _____ a waiter during the summer holidays. It was awful We had to work _____ slaves and some of the customers treated us _____ dirt.

2 *A* He's hoping to get a job _____ a racing driver.
B Well, he'll be better _____ a Grand Prix driver than he is on the road. He drives _____ a lunatic.

·3 *A* I don't think you should marry him, Kathy. I don't want to interfere; I'm speaking _____ a friend.
B Well, you talk _____ my father.

4 *A* He works _____ a lorry driver.
B Does he? Well, the only thing I know about him is that he eats _____ a horse and drinks _____ a fish.

5 He started collecting stamps _____ a hobby but he's since developed it _____ a full-time job. It's the only thing he does.

42 **not so much, more (like) . . . than, rather . . . than**

a
Compare these sentences:

He's **not so much** an actor **as** a singer.
He's **more (like)** a singer **than** an actor.
He's a singer, **rather than** an actor.

Rewrite these sentences, using two alternative forms given in the examples above:

1 It's not so much a play as a dramatised novel.
2 It was more his brother's fault than his.
3 It's a cottage, rather than a country house.
4 He's more like an accountant than a secretary.
5 They're not so much neighbours as friends, as far as we're concerned.

b
Compare these sentences:

What destroyed the English wine industry was **not so much** a change in the climate **as** the competition from France.
The competition from France, **rather than** a change in the climate, was what destroyed the English wine industry.

Rewrite these sentences, using the alternative form given in the examples above:

1 It was not so much his selfishness as his bad manners that annoyed me.

2 What causes the majority of accidents is not so much the quality of the cars as the carelessness of a lot of drivers.

3 The main danger facing the Olympic movement is the lack of common sense among the organisers, rather than political interference.

Modals and auxiliaries

43   can, could

Look at this passage and dialogue about Anne. The information comes from the table below.

Anne **could** swim when she was six. She **could** ride a bicycle when she was eight. She **could** read music when she was ten but she **couldn't** play the piano. She **can** type but she **can't** drive a car.

A   **Can** she type?
B   Yes, she **can**.
A   **Can** she drive a car?
B   No, she **can't**.
A   **Could** she swim when she was seven?
B   Yes, she **could**.
A   **Could** she ride a bicycle?
B   No, she **couldn't**.
A   What **could** she do when she was fourteen?
B   She **could** swim, ride a bicycle, read music and play the piano. But she **couldn't** type or drive a car.

Name	Age when she learnt to:					
	swim	ride a bicycle	read music	play the piano	type	drive a car
Anne	6	8	10	11	15	–
Barbara	7	9	–	–	16	17
Claire	8	7	12	13	17	–
Dinah	–	6	9	10	–	18

1   Make questions, like those above, to ask Barbara about what she can and could do. Write down her answers, using the information in the table,

      e.g.   *A*   **Can you play the piano?**
            B   **No, I can't.**

2   Write a paragraph like the one above about Anne for Claire.
Write in the first person, beginning **I could** . . .

3   Write a paragraph like the one above about Anne for Dinah. Write in the third person, beginning **Dinah could** . . .

44   can, will be able to

Compare these sentences:

Can I have an ice-cream please?
Will your grandfather **be able to** climb the stairs?

In the first sentence, the speaker is asking for permission. In the second sentence, the speaker asks if it will be possible for the old man to climb the stairs.

Look at this dialogue:

Terry broke his leg playing football yesterday. Now he is in hospital and his leg is in plaster.

Terry   **Can** I get up this afternoon?
Doctor Of course you **can't**.
Terry   **Can** my friends come to see me?
Doctor Yes, they **can** come this evening.
Terry   When **will** I **be able to** get up?
Doctor Quite soon. You **won't be able to** walk immediately but you'll **be able to** go round on crutches.

Complete these dialogues with **can**, **can't** or **will/won't be able to** and a main verb. The first letter of each main verb is given.

a *Terry is talking to the doctor.*

Terry   ___1___ I t__1__ the radio on?
Doctor Yes, of course you ___2___.
Terry   ___3___ I g__3__ downstairs and watch the football match on TV?
Doctor No, I'm sorry. You ___4___.
Terry   ___5___ my girl-friend c__5__ to see me this evening?
Doctor Yes, she ___6___.
Terry   ___7___ she s__7__ the night here?
Doctor Of course she ___8___. This is a hospital, not a hotel.
Terry   When ___9___ I w__9__?
Doctor I don't know yet. I ___10___ t__10__ you when we take the plaster off.

b *Terry is talking to his girl-friend Karen.*

Karen   Hello, Terry. ___1___ I w__1__ my name on your plaster?
Terry   You ___2___ if you like.
Karen   When are they going to take it off?
Terry   The doctor thinks they ___3___ t__3__ it off next week. But I ___4___ p__4__ football again for two months.
Karen   Oh! ___5___ you d__5__? There's a dance at the club next weekend.
Terry   Of course I ___6___ d__6__! I can't walk yet, so I ___7___ d__7__, ___7___ I?
Karen   Oh. ___8___ I g__8__ to the dance without you?
Terry   With Johnny Bradshaw? No, you ___9___.

    Karen   That's not fair. You say I __10__ d __10__ because you've got a broken leg. You're selfish.

    Terry   All right, Karen. You __11__ g __11__ to the dance. But I __12__ g __12__ too, because the doctor says I __13__ w __13__ on my crutches. So I __14__ t __14__ you to the dance and w __14__ you dancing, and if Johnny Bradshaw dances too close, I __15__ h __15__ him with my crutch, __15__ I?

45 **can, be able to, be capable of**

a **to be able to**
Look at these sentences:

He **can** play the piano beautifully. I'd like **to be able to** play as well as he does.

Can is an auxiliary and the infinitive form is **to be able to**.

Use **to be able to** to complete these sentences:
1. It would be lovely _____ lie on the beach all day but I have a lot of work to do.
2. He couldn't come to this meeting but he hopes _____ attend the next one.
3. It's too soon for you to think of driving a car. After the accident you had, you're lucky _____ walk, let alone drive.
4. I'd like _____ swim as well as she can.
5. We can't give you the results of the experiment today, but we expect _____ announce them next week.

b **have/haven't been able to**
Look at this sentence:

I played tennis a lot last year, but this year I **haven't been able to** spare the time.

The Present Perfect tense exists in the form **have been able to**.

Use **have been able to** and **haven't been able to** to complete these sentences:
1. The police have been looking for the murderer for three months but they _____ catch him yet.
2. I had terrible mathematics teachers at school and as a result I _____ never _____ understand geometry.
3. He said there were five copies in the library but I've been looking for half an hour and I _____ only _____ find two.
4. By means of X-rays, scientists _____ demonstrate that King Arthur's round table was actually made about 1330.
5. I've rung him several times but I _____ contact him.

able to, capable of

Compare these sentences:

> The adder is the only British snake **able to kill** a man.
> The adder is the only British snake **capable of killing** a man.
>
> It is said that George Washington was **unable to tell** a lie.
> It is said that George Washington was **incapable of telling** a lie.

Able and **capable**, **unable** and **incapable** are similar in meaning but note the difference in construction. **Able to** is followed by an infinitive; **capable of** is followed by a gerund.

In the sentences below, replace the words in italics with a phrase using **capable of** or **incapable of**:

> e.g. He *can drink* fifteen pints of beer in an evening.
>   He **is capable of drinking** fifteen pints of beer in an evening.

1 I don't think I would be *able to kill* anyone, even in self-defence. I haven't got a violent temperament.
2 When the installation is complete, the factory will be *able to produce* 1000 tons a day and we expect it to do so.
3 He *can argue* for hours if you give him the opportunity to do so.
4 He is the only man I know who *can drink* a bottle of whisky in an evening, and he often does so.
5 He would be hopeless as a managing director. He *can't make up his mind* about anything. He always asks someone else.
6 I'm sure John didn't do it. He *would never behave* so badly. He's such a good boy.

> NOTE   **Able** and **capable of** are not always exactly the same in meaning. **Capable of** often means 'able to and likely to',
>   e.g. **He is capable of committing a crime.** (He is not only able to commit a crime if he has the opportunity, but he is the kind of person who would take the opportunity.)
>   For **can**, **could** and **will be able to**, see Practices 43 and 44.

46 **may, might**

Notice the use of **may** and **might** in these sentences:

> *Roger and Carol are at the casino.*

Roger   I'm going to bet on the red. It **may** win. (Perhaps it will win – the chances are about 50/50.)

Carol   But it **may not**. The black **may** win. I'm going to bet on one of the numbers, number 11.

Roger   Then you're almost certain to lose. You have only one chance in 36.

Carol   I **might not**. Number 11 **might** win. (It's unlikely, but possible.)

Note that **can** is only used for possibility when we are talking about what is possible at all times, not one particular time,

e.g. **Accidents can happen.**

But in giving a particular person advice, whether or not he is driving at the time, we would say,

e.g. **Drive carefully. You may (might) have an accident.**

Complete these sentences with **may (not)** or **might (not)**. Choose **might (not)** only if you think the possibility is very remote:

Mr Pryor, an insurance salesman, knocks on Adam's door one morning, trying to sell insurance.

Mr Pryor   Good morning. I represent the Beacon Insurance Company. You ___1___ be fully insured, so I'd like to talk to you about our policies.

Adam   Well, I'm not insured, actually.

Mr Pryor   Ah, well, you ___2___ be sorry about that one day. For instance, your wife and children ___3___ be left in difficult circumstances.

Adam   But I'm not married.

Mr Pryor   But you're still young, sir. You ___4___ get married quite soon. You ___5___ even meet the lady on your way to work this morning.

Adam   Well, I ___6___, but it's not very likely, is it? On the other hand, I ___7___ miss my train if I stand here talking to you.

Mr Pryor   You ___8___ be sorry if you don't sir. You say this flat isn't insured?

Adam   Well, no, it isn't.

Mr Pryor   Good heavens! Thieves ___9___ break in while you're out. They ___10___ even break in today. Of course, they ___11___, but it's better to be safe than sorry.

Adam   Well, you ___12___ be right. I'd better take your telephone number.

Mr Pryor   I'd rather make an appointment to see you, sir. I travel a lot in my job, so I ___13___ be at the office when you ring.

47   **may have, might have**

Compare these sentences:

A   Where's the cake?

B   The children **may have eaten** it. (Perhaps they have eaten it.)

A   Where's the cake?

B   Someone **might have stolen** it. (Perhaps someone has stolen it.)

May have and **might have** are used to express the possibility that something happened in the past. They can be used in place of both the Present Perfect and the Past Simple when we are not sure what <u>has happened</u> or what <u>happened</u>. We use **might have** when something is less likely to have happened.

1 Rewrite the following sentences, using **may have** in 1–4 and **might have** in 5–8:

Flora wonders why her husband, Tom, is late coming home from work. She thinks of the following possibilities:

1 The trains from London are sometimes delayed.
2 Tom sometimes has to work late and then he misses his usual train.
3 Sometimes he goes for a drink after work with some friends.
4 Sometimes he takes clients out to dinner. In that case, he usually telephones in the afternoon, but I was out for most of the time.

Flora is worried and considers these unlikely possibilities:

5 Perhaps the train has crashed.
6 Perhaps Tom has had an accident.
7 Perhaps he has been knocked down by a car.
8 Perhaps he has taken his secretary to the cinema.

2 Rewrite the following possibilities using **may have** in 1–3 and **might have** in 4–6:

When Tom arrives home about 7 o'clock (he stopped to talk to an old friend he met on the train), Flora asks him, 'Where's your umbrella?' He considers these possibilities:

e.g.   Did I leave it at the office?
  I may have left it at the office.

1 Did I put it down when I bought my ticket at the station?
2 Did I leave it on the train?
3 Did I rest it against the wall when I was talking to Arthur?

Then he thinks of some less likely possibilities:

e.g.   Did it fall under the seat in the train compartment?
  It might have fallen under the seat in the train compartment.

4 Did Arthur take it by mistake?
5 Did the boss borrow it when he went out this afternoon?
6 Did I drop it in the street?

Then he remembers it was a sunny morning. He may not have taken it to the office. He may not have lost it. And in fact it is standing in its place in the hall.

48   **must, mustn't, needn't, don't have to, don't need to**

Look at these sentences:

I **must** remember to post that letter. It's very important.
You **must** do your homework. If you don't, you'll fail the examination.
He **has to** get up early every morning. He starts work at seven.

If you want to go from Oxford to Newark by train, you **have to** change trains three times.

You **mustn't** drive after you have been drinking alcohol.

I **needn't** go to work today. The boss said I could have the day off.

I **don't have to/don't need to** go to work on Saturdays. (The office is closed.)

Must and **have to** are very similar in meaning. They both indicate an obligation to do something, but see NOTE below.

Mustn't (or **must not**) is used for an obligation <u>not</u> to do something.

Needn't, **don't have to** and **don't need to** all mean that there is no obligation to do something.

Use **must**, **mustn't** or **needn't** in each space to complete the following dialogue:

Mr Jones is in hospital. The doctor has just come to see him.

Doctor   You've had a very serious operation, Mr Jones. Now you ___1___ rest. You ___2___ do anything that would tire you.

Mr Jones   Can I get up?

Doctor   No, you ___3___ get up yet. You ___4___ stay in bed until Saturday. But you ___5___ lie there doing nothing. You can read a book, if you like. But you ___6___ start doing work from the office.

Mr Jones   Oh, dear. There's so much work to do. I ___7___ start soon.

Doctor   You ___8___ be foolish, Mr Jones. The office will go on without you, so you ___9___ worry about it. In fact your boss rang me up this morning to ask how you were. 'Everything's all right,' he said, 'Jones ___10___ come back for a month.' I was very annoyed with him. 'Mr Smith,' I said, 'my patient ___11___ go back to work for a month. It would be very dangerous.' He understood my point of view so you ___12___ worry about your salary. He'll pay it until you are better.

Mr Jones   Thank you, Doctor. Do I need to continue with the same drugs?

Doctor   Well, you ___13___ take the blue pills as before, but you ___14___ continue with the red ones – they aren't necessary. And another thing, you ___15___ open the windows. You ___16___ get some fresh air. It's too hot in here. Of course you ___17___ stand in front of the window and catch cold, but I ___18___ tell you that. That's just common sense. I'll be back to see you on Saturday.

NOTE **Must** and **have to** are not exactly the same in meaning. **Must** is used for an obligation that is imposed by the speaker, as in the first two examples above. **Have to** is used for an obligation that comes from outside, for example from an employer or a transport system, as in the second two examples above.

Very often **must** and **have to** are interchangeable and the choice depends on whether the speaker feels that the obligation is personal or imposed by circumstances,

e.g.   **I must/have to clean the house today.**
Is the speaker cleaning the house because he or she has an obligation to himself or herself, or because the house needs it?

49   must, should, ought to, mustn't, shouldn't, ought not to

a   **must, should, ought to**

Compare these sentences:

You **must** stop at the red light.
You **should/ought to** be polite to other people.

Must is used for an obligation that is felt personally. It is used if the person in the situation has a legal obligation to do something or will really suffer if he doesn't do it.

Should (or **ought to**) is used if it is just a sensible or good thing to do. The same differences exist in the negative.

Complete these sentences with **must** or **should**:

1   You _____ sign your name on the contract but you _____ read it first.
2   You _____ give up smoking. If you don't, it will kill you.
3   You _____ smoke cigars or a pipe. They're not so bad for you.
4   I _____ buy a new watch. This one is broken.
5   You _____ buy a new watch. That one's very old.
6   A   You _____ answer all the questions.
    B   All of them?
    A   Yes, the exam paper says so, but it doesn't say you _____ answer them in order. You _____ leave any questions you can't answer until the end, and then come back to them.

Substitute **ought to** in those sentences above where you have written **should**.

b   **mustn't, shouldn't, ought not to**

Compare these sentences:

You **mustn't** throw stones at other children. (because you will make them suffer, and you will also break the law)
You **shouldn't/ought not to** say unkind things to other children. (It's not nice, but it's not illegal and I can't stop you.)

Complete the sentences with **mustn't** or **shouldn't**:

1 You _____ smoke in the cinema. Can't you see the notice?
2 You _____ talk in the cinema. You'll annoy people.
3 You _____ let the baby crawl all over the floor. He'll get dirty.
4 You _____ let the baby put his finger in the light socket. It's very dangerous.
5 I _____ tell anyone about this, because it's a secret, but I'll tell you, because you're my closest friend – Bob and Jill are getting a divorce. But you _____ tell anyone else. Jill would be furious with me if she knew.
6 He _____ eat chocolate with sugar in it, because he's a diabetic. I _____ eat sweets, either, because they make me fat, but I can't resist the temptation.
7 You _____ turn the TV on so loud. You'll wake the baby.
8 You _____ turn the TV on so loud. It's not fair to the neighbours.

Substitute **ought not to** in those sentences above where you have written **shouldn't**.

50 **must, can't** (to express a logical deduction)

a **must**

Look at these sentences:

It's getting dark. **It must be about seven o'clock.**
You've been working hard all day. **You must feel tired.**

Must (not **have to**) is used when we are almost certain something is true because our logic tells us so.

Use **must** and the words in brackets to make a sentence, as in the example, about each of these sentences:

e.g. Brian has a good job. He's got a big house and an expensive car. (earn . . . money)
He must earn a lot of money.

1 The ashtrays in Colin's house are always full of cigarette ends. (smoke . . . cigarettes)
2 Dora wears different clothes every day. (have . . . clothes)
3 Eric spends every evening in the pub. (drink . . . beer)
4 Flora plays tennis very well. (win . . . matches)
5 Gordon is a translator at the United Nations. He translates for people from different countries. (speak . . . languages)
6 Harry is a car salesman. His firm is very pleased with him. (sell . . . cars)
7 Ingrid goes to cocktail parties every week. (meet . . . people)
8 Julian's car is very big and old. (use . . . petrol)

b **can't**

Look at these sentences:

> Gerald arrives at his office at 11 o'clock and always plays golf after lunch. **He can't do much work.**
>
> Anne is always nervous when she plays tennis. **She can't win many games.**
>
> The opposite of **must** in this sense is **can't**. It expresses a certainty that something is not true.

Use **can't** and the words in brackets to make a sentence, as in the example, about each of these sentences:

> e.g.   Philip is a terrible painter. (sell . . . pictures)
> **He can't sell many pictures.**
> 1   Queenie always wears the same dress. (have . . . clothes)
> 2   Roger saves half of what he earns. (spend . . . money)
> 3   Susan is always alone. (have . . . friends)
> 4   Terry's telephone bill was only £3. (make . . . calls)
> 5   Ursula never smiles. (be . . . happy)
> 6   Victor's students don't know anything. (be . . . good teacher)
> 7   William's room is always in a mess. (be . . . tidy)
> 8   Xenophon's dog always runs away when it sees a cat. (be . . . brave dog)
> 9   Yolanda always eats tinned food. (be . . . good cook)

51   **must have, should have, ought to have**

Compare these sentences:

> He's late. He **must have missed** the train.
> Oh, no! I've missed the train! I **should have/ought to have left** home five minutes earlier.
>
> **Must have** + past participle is the past tense form of **must** when it expresses a logical conclusion about a past action. (Compare Practice 50.) **Should have** or **ought to have** + past participle are used when we talk about what we were going to do, or were supposed to do, but for some reason did not do.

Read the story below about Harry's Monday morning. Find a reason why different things went wrong, and imagine what Harry said to himself about the things he was supposed to do, using **must have**:

> e.g.   **I must have forgotten to set the alarm last night.**
> I had a terrible morning today. Everything went wrong. First, I was going to get up at 7.00, because a customer was coming to the office at 9.00. But I didn't wake up in time. I suppose I forgot to set the alarm last night. Then I was going to shave. But I couldn't find my razor. I

suppose I left it at Jack's yesterday. I intended to catch the 8.00 train, so I ran to the station, but when I got there I hadn't got my season ticket. I suppose I put it in my other jacket. So I was going to buy a ticket, but I hadn't brought my wallet, either. I suppose it was in my other jacket, too. In the end I borrowed some money from a neighbour who was at the station and caught the 8.30 train. I was due to see the customer at 9.00 but when I got to the office he wasn't there. I suppose he thought I wasn't coming.

2   Now read the story again. Notice the things which Harry intended to do, was going to do, or was due to do but which he didn't do. Write them down, using **should have** or **ought to have**:

e.g.   **He should have got up at 7.00.**

52   **had to, must have**

a   **had to**

Look at these sentences:

I **had to** take my car to the garage yesterday.
A   **Did you have to** do a lot of work for the exam?
B   No, it was very easy. I **didn't have to** do much at all.

Had to is in almost all cases the past tense form of **must** (when it is used to mean obligation) and **have to**.
The question and negative forms are made with **did**. **Didn't have to** means that there is no obligation. When we want to express the idea of something being forbidden, we use **was/were not allowed to**.

Read through the following and answer the questions at the end:

Mrs Cooper has a new cleaning woman called Doreen. Before she leaves the house in the morning she gives her some instructions:

I want you to: do the washing-up.
       make the beds.
       put the dirty clothes in the washing machine and wash them.
       do the ironing.
       give the cat its milk.
But you mustn't: smoke.
       play the record-player.
       open the drinks cupboard.
       invite any of your friends in.
       use the telephone.
1   What did Doreen have to do?
2   What wasn't she allowed to do?

b   **must have**

A   He couldn't find it when he arrived at the office.
B   He **must have dropped** it on the way.

Must have + past participle is the past tense form of **must** when it expresses a logical conclusion about a past action.

The negative is formed with **can't have** (normally Present Perfect), and **couldn't have** (normally Past Simple) + past participle (compare Practice 50),

e.g.   *A*   He says he's lost it.

      B   He **can't have lost** it. I've only just given it to him.

Read the following and make sentences, using **must have**, as in the example below:

When Mrs Cooper came home, Doreen was not there, but the house was in a mess. Doreen had done everything she was supposed to do badly and she had done everything she wasn't allowed to do.

e.g.   There were a lot of cigarette ends in the ashtray.

      She must have smoked a lot of cigarettes.

1   One of the records was scratched.
2   The whisky bottle was empty.
3   There were four dirty glasses on the table.
4   There were some telephone numbers written down next to the telephone.

53 **Did you have to?**

Notice the verb form in this question:

      Did you have to go to hospital?

Complete the conversation, using the correct question form **did you have to**; put in an appropriate verb where one is not given:

Bill Lord has just come home from work. He tells his wife, Betty, he's had a terrible day. He's had to deal with one problem after another.

BETTY	BILL
e.g. **What did you have to do?**	First I had to visit a customer.
Did you have to go by car?	Yes.
1 Where _____?	To Walton.
2 Who _____?	Mr Black. But he was busy. So I had to wait.
3 How long _____?	About half an hour. And after the interview, I went down to the car and there was a policeman there. The car was blocking the entrance.
4 _____ move it?	Yes, but then Mr Black's secretary came down, so I had to leave it. The policeman was very annoyed.
5 _____ go back upstairs?	Yes.

6	What _____ do?	I had to see the Advertising Manager. And when I got back, they had taken the car to the car pound.
7	_____ there to collect it?	Yes.
8	_____ pay a fine?	Yes, £20. But that wasn't the end of it. On the way back to the office I ran out of petrol.
9	_____ push the car to a garage?	No. I left it on the road and walked.
10	How far _____?	Two miles.
11	_____ walk back, too?	Yes. Four miles altogether. My feet are killing me.

54 have had to, had had to, would have to, would have had to

Look at these sentences:

> I've had to work hard all my life.
> When I saw the door was locked, I thought I would have to break a window to get in.
> If I hadn't had to leave school at fourteen, I would have been able to complete my studies and I wouldn't have had to accept such a dull job.

Have to can be used in the Present Perfect, Past Perfect, Conditional and Conditional Perfect. Must cannot be used as an alternative. (See also Practices 48 and 51.)

Use the correct forms of have/has/had to, had had to, would have to or would have had to to complete the following sentences:

1 If I had a better job, my wife _____ (negative) go out to work.
2 A Have you heard about the Browns? They _____ sell their car.
  B Why?
  A Well, it seems Mr Brown bets on horses and he got into debt. If Mr Brown's father hadn't lent them some money, they _____ sell their house, as well. I'm glad my husband doesn't gamble.
3 A I'm very pleased with the second-hand car I bought. I _____ (negative) take it back to the garage for servicing and I've already been driving it for six months.
  B I did eight thousand miles with mine, and if I _____ (negative) change the tyres, I wouldn't have sold it, either.
4 My leg has been bothering me again, Doctor. I _____ stay at home and my husband _____ do the shopping. It's a bit better today. Otherwise, I _____ ask you to visit me at home. I couldn't have come to the surgery.

5 *A* It's a pity you missed the film.

   B Yes, I'd like to have seen it. If I _____ (negative) work late at the office, I'd have come with you. I _____ work late three times this week and I'm getting tired of it. But the boss warned us that we _____ do overtime until this job was finished.

55 Shall I? Will I?

Compare these sentences:

Shall I get you an aspirin?
Will I get a good mark in the exam?

Note that **Shall I?** here means 'Would you like me to?' In most cases in modern English there is no difference between **shall** and **will** in the first person, and in spoken English we usually say **I'll**. **Will** is becoming much more common than **shall** in normal future statements in the first person,

e.g. If they attack us, **we shall/will** resist them.
But note that in questions, **Shall I/we?** is the only correct form when you mean 'Would you like me/us to?'

e.g. *A* **Shall I** open the window?
    B Yes, please. It's very hot in here.

or in sentences like:

What **shall I** do? (What do you think I should do?)

Use **shall** to complete these sentences only when it is necessary. Use **will** in the other sentences:

1 *A* _____ I help you with those cases?
  B Yes, please. They're very heavy.
2 *A* _____ I live to be a hundred, Doctor?
  B Not if you go on smoking fifty cigarettes a day.
3 *A* If Mr Jones comes while you're out, what _____ I say to him?
  B Tell him I'll ring him tomorrow.
4 *A* What _____ we do with the drunken sailor?
  B Pour cold water on him.
5 *A* _____ we get home in time to see the film on TV?
  B Yes, if you hurry.

56 had better

Look at these sentences:

A I don't feel very well.
B Then **you'd better** see the doctor.

I feel very tired. **I'd better** go to bed.
He looks angry. **I'd better not** interrupt him.

The boss would be annoyed if he saw you doing that. **You'd better not** do it again.

Had better is used to mean 'I think I/you/he, etc. should . . .'
or 'It would be sensible/right if I/you/he, etc. . . .'
In the same way, the negative form **had better not** is used to mean 'I think I/you/he, etc. shouldn't . . .' or 'It wouldn't be sensible/right if I/you/he, etc. . . .'

Add a second sentence to each one given here using **I'd better** and the words in brackets:

1 I'm tired of sitting at home all day. (get a job)
2 I think one of the pipes is leaking. (ring the plumber)
3 I've got a terrible cough. (stop smoking)
4 I've lost my passport. (go to the consulate)
5 I'm getting fat. (take up yoga)

Add a second sentence to each one given here, using **you'd better**, **he'd better**, etc. and the words in brackets:

6 I don't know the way to the station. (ask a policeman)
7 I've got a headache. (take an aspirin)
8 They want to go to the theatre, but the play's very popular. (book the tickets in advance)
9 You've upset her by saying that. (apologise to her)
10 I want to make a will. (see a solicitor)

Write a sentence before each one given here using **I'd better not** and the words given in brackets:

11 (say anything about it now) She might hear us.
12 (turn the record player up) The neighbours might object.
13 (drink any more) My head's going round.
14 (argue with him) He's bigger than me.
15 (promise I can come) I've got a lot of work to do next week.

Add a second sentence to each one given here, or write one before it using **you'd better not**, **he'd better not**, etc. and the words in brackets:

16 The boss is in a bad mood. (keep him waiting)
17 They always made fun of their last teacher. (behave like that with me)
18 What are you doing up that apple tree? (let the farmer see you)
19 (lend him the money) He may not pay you back.
20 (wear that dress) She'll get it dirty.

57 used to, used not to

Look at these sentences:

When I was at school, I **used to** study every night. (but now I go out and have a good time)

I **used not to** smoke when I was at school. (but now I smoke 20 cigarettes a day)

Used to appears as a past form in contrast to the present to express what we habitually did, but do not do now.

Note that **didn't use to** is now accepted as an alternative to **used not to**.

Used to and **used not to** are always followed by the infinitive. They cannot be used in a present form; we use the Present Simple tense instead,

e.g.   I **smoke** 20 cigarettes a day.

I **don't study** these days.

In the sentences below, replace the Past Simple tense (in italics) with a form of **used to**:

Tom Green has just returned to the small town where he used to live. A lot of things have changed in the past thirty years. He says to his wife:

e.g.   When I was a boy, I *played* football twice a week.

When I was a boy, I **used to play** football twice a week.

1 There *was* a market in the centre of the town, where the supermarket is now. The farmers *came* in from the country every week to sell their produce.

2 Look at that new housing estate. There *was* a field there. We *played* football on it.

3 We *went* to the cinema every Saturday morning, but now it's a Bingo hall.

4 And I *bought* bread at the baker's shop on the corner but now it's a big store.

5 And look at the buses! They're red. They *were* painted green.

6 The streets are full of cars, too. There *wasn't* much traffic then.

7 And there *weren't* any traffic lights or zebra crossings, either.

8 They've built a lot of flats, too. People *didn't live* in flats in this town. They *lived* in small houses.

9 And they *worked* on the land. There *weren't* any factories.

58 would rather

a I'd rather

Notice the use of **I'd rather** (**I would rather**) in these sentences:

A Would you like some tea?

B **I'd rather** have coffee, if it's no trouble.

    A Would you like an apple?
    B **I'd rather** have an orange, if you don't mind.

1 Make questions and answers in the same way with the following:
    1 wine/beer 2 red wine/white wine 3 a glass of milk/a glass of beer 4 a boiled egg/an omelette 5 strawberries/raspberries

Here is another example of **would rather**:

    A Would you like to play tennis on Saturday?
    B Well, **I'd rather** play on Sunday, if you don't mind.

2 Make questions and answers in the same way with the following:
    1 go to the theatre with me on Friday (Saturday) 2 go to the circus with me next week (to the zoo) 3 listen to some records (watch the TV) 4 play chess (play cards) 5 ride my motor-bike (sit on the back)

b **Would you rather?**
Notice the question form:

    A **Would you rather** have tea or coffee?
    B Tea, please.

Make questions and answers in the same way with the following:
    1 cheese/cake 2 ice cream/fruit salad 3 boiled potatoes/chips 4 grapefruit/yogurt 5 (listen to) a classical record/a jazz record

c **I'd rather not**
Notice that we don't need to repeat the main verb after **I'd rather not**:

    A Would you like to play tennis on Saturday?
    B Well, **I'd rather not** (play) if you don't mind. I'd like to watch the football match on TV. How about Sunday?

Make questions and answers in the same way with the following:
1 go to the cinema with me tomorrow – have got to do some work – Wednesday
2 come round for a drink this evening – am very busy – tomorrow
3 watch the game on TV – don't like football much – the play this evening
4 go for a walk – feel tired – playing chess.
5 have lunch with me on Tuesday – have got to go to the dentist – Friday

NOTE If we make a comparison about what we **would rather have** at any one moment, we say,

e.g. **I'd rather have coffee than tea.**

If we are talking in general terms, we can either use the same form or say,

e.g. **I prefer coffee to tea.**

69 **So do I, I do, too,** etc.

Look at these sentences, noticing the word order of the responses:

A I like apples.
B **I do, too. / So do I.**

A He plays tennis very well.
B **His sister does, too. / So does his sister.**

A They worked very hard yesterday.
B **We did, too. / So did we.**

A I've passed the exam.
B **John has, too. / So has John.**

A They're going on holiday soon.
B **We are, too. / So are we.**

Notice that with **so** the auxiliary (**do, did, have,** etc.) and its subject are inverted.

Now look at the sentences below and make two responses for each of them, using the words in brackets:

e.g. My father smokes cigars. (mine)
     So does mine. / Mine does, too.
1 He gets up at 7 o'clock every morning. (I)
2 They lived in London when they were young. (we)
3 She's getting married next week. (my brother)
4 I've lost my ticket. (I)
5 I'll be late if I don't hurry. (we)
6 I was tired of listening to him playing the piano. (the neighbours)
7 You're always bad-tempered in the morning. (you)
8 My father can swim five kilometres. (mine)
9 I eat honey every day. (my wife)
10 She starts singing as soon as she wakes up. (the birds)

Verb forms

60 Present Continuous, **going to** Future

Look at this conversation:

Angela	We**'re having** a party on Saturday.
Jean	Oh, who**'s coming**?
Angela	I don't know yet, but we**'re going to invite** all our friends. Would you like to come?
Jean	I'd love to, but I**'m going away** this weekend.

We prefer to use the Present Continuous tense in future time instead of **going to** when we have already planned something and it is not just an intention. In such cases there is usually a future time expression in the sentence (e.g. **next week, tomorrow**). We also prefer the Present Continuous tense with verbs like **come** and **go** (to avoid saying 'going to come').

Put the verb in brackets into the Present Continuous tense if the action has already been arranged. If the action is not obviously planned, use the **going to** form:

a	*Mary*	Jack and Jill (1. get) married on Saturday. Her brother Andrew (2. come) all the way from Scotland for the wedding. He (3. leave) Edinburgh on Friday. It's a long drive so he (4. look for) a hotel near Birmingham. He (5. spend) the night there and (6. finish) the journey the next morning. I (7. buy) the wedding present this afternoon. Would you like to come with me?
	Paula	All right. I (8. go) into town this afternoon. What (9. buy) you?
	Mary	I'm not sure. Something useful. Jack and Jill haven't got much money so they (10. need) a lot of things for the house.
b	*Paul*	We (1. go) to the New Forest for a picnic on Sunday. We (2. look for) a nice place under the trees. Then we (3. sit down) and eat our lunch.
	Linda	Are you (4. take) all the food with you?
	Paul	Yes. Mum (5. make) some sandwiches and my Uncle Jack (6. bring) all the drinks. He (7. come), too, with my cousins, Peter and Jenny. We (8. play) games in the forest. I (9. be) Robin Hood. Would you like to come with us? You can be Maid Marian.
	Linda	Oh yes. But my Aunt Rachel (10. arrive) on Saturday. We (11. meet) her at the station. She's awful. She (12. spend) all weekend talking about her illnesses. She always does. She (13. have) an operation next month, Mum says.
	Paul	Is it serious?
	Linda	No. She only (14. have) her tonsils out. I (15. go) home now. I (16. ask) my mother if she'll let me come with you.

61 Verbs not used in Continuous forms

Look at these sentences:

Listen! I **hear** bells ringing.
Do you **remember** her name?
No meat, thank you. I **don't like** pork.

Note that the Present Simple is used here although these sentences refer to the present moment, when we would normally use the Present Continuous. A number of common verbs are not usually used in continuous (progressive) tenses; the Present Simple will be used when we refer to the present as well as when we refer to general truths. Here is a list of these verbs:

hear, see, smell, taste (these are often used with **can**);
notice, recognise, believe, feel (that), think (that);
forget, remember, know, mean, suppose, understand;
dislike, hate, like, love, want, wish;
appear (when it means 'seem'), **seem**;
belong to, contain, matter.

Note that **think** meaning 'have in one's mind', can also be used in combination forms,

e.g. **What do you think?** (What is your opinion?)
Do you think (that) he's good-looking? (Is it your opinion that he's good-looking?)
but:
What are you thinking about? (What is in your mind at this moment?)

Use one of the verbs from the list above to complete each space in this dialogue, but do not use any of them more than once; in a few cases, more than one verb would be possible. Use negative and question forms where indicated. The first letter of each verb is given to help you:

Steele I'm sure I r___1___ you. I never f___2___ a face and yours s___3___ very familiar.

Robb I b___4___ (negative) we've ever met. I t___5___ you've made a mistake.

Steele I s___6___ you're right. But I u___7___ (negative) it. I r___8___ your face. I w___9___ (negative) to be a nuisance because I h___10___ annoying people but have you ever been in prison?

Robb What? What m___11___ you (question)? I k___12___ (negative) what you're talking about.

Steele Well, it m___13___ (negative). Naturally you l___14___ (negative) people reminding you of it. But before you go, that watch b___15___ me.

Robb Which watch?

Steele The one you took out of my pocket when we started talking. A thief like me n___16___ these things. And I recognise another thief when I see one.

62   Present Continuous with **always**

Compare these sentences:

I always (sometimes, never) catch colds in winter.
I'**m always catching** colds.

Those children always (usually, never) scream when it's time to go to bed.
Those children **are always screaming**.

Always (but not other frequency adverbs, e.g. **sometimes**, etc.) is used with the Present Continuous tense to suggest 'more often than we would like or expect', so it usually expresses some kind of complaint. Unlike the use of frequency adverbs with the Present Simple tense, this form is not usually connected to a time expression, e.g. **in winter**, **when it's time to go to bed**.

Choose the most appropriate tense for the verbs in brackets in these sentences:

1   He always (go) to work by bus.
2   You always (work)! Why don't you have a rest from time to time?
3   They always (grumble) when the food is cold.
4   He always (grumble). I'm tired of listening to his complaints.
5   She always (smile) when she sees me.
6   She always (smile). I don't see what she's so happy about.
7   He always (play) golf on Sundays.
8   He always (play) golf. Doesn't he ever do any work?
9   They always (go) on strike. It's not surprising the factory makes a loss.
10 They always (go) on strike just before Christmas to cause as much trouble as they can.

63   Present Perfect Simple and Continuous

Compare these sentences:

Leighton City **have been playing** badly this season.
                              for two months.
                              since the season started.
They **have lost** five games and **have** only **won** one.
They **haven't won** a game for two months.
                              since August.

Notice that the Present Perfect Continuous, **have been playing** is used for an action that has continued for a period of time.

Look at these tables which give the playing record of the forward line and the football club's playing record this season:

Name	Joined club	In first team	Goals this season
ALLAN	1976	1978	4
BENNETT	1973	1977	3
CURTIS	1975	1976	2
DALE	1978	1979	1
EMERY	1971	1974	1

Leighton City Football Club's results – 1980–1 season

When played	Played against	Result	Scorers
August 25th	ATHLETIC (H)	won 2–1	Allan, Bennett
September 1st	WANDERERS (H)	lost 2–3	Curtis, Bennett
September 8th	ALBION (A)	lost 3–4	Emery, Bennett, Allan
September 15th	TOWN (A)	drew 2–2	Allan, Dale
September 22nd	RANGERS (H)	lost 2–4	Curtis, Allan
September 29th	PARK (A)	drew 0–0	
October 6th	CELTIC (H)	lost 0–2	
October 13th	BOROUGH (A)	lost 0–1	

H = played at home   A = played away

Use the information in the first table to ask and answer these questions about each player. There are two ways of answering the questions, one with **for** and one with **since**:

1 How long has he been playing for the club?
2 How long has he been playing for the first team?
  e.g. **Allan has been playing for the club for __ years/ since 1976.**
       He's been playing for the first team for __ years/since 1978.
3 How many goals has he scored this season?
4 How long is it since he scored a goal?
  e.g. **He's scored 4 goals this season.**
       He hasn't scored for __ weeks/since August 25th.

Use the information in the second table to answer these questions about Leighton City Football Club. There are two ways of answering the questions, one with **for** and one with **since**:

5 How many games has the club won this season?
6 How many have they lost?
7 How many have they drawn?
8 How long is it since they won a game/drew a game/scored a goal?
  e.g. **They haven't won a game for __ weeks/since August 25th.**

64 Present Perfect with **ever** and **never**

Compare these sentences:

I've never been in a casino **before**.
It's **the first time I've ever been** in a casino.

Rewrite these sentences, using the alternative form with **ever** or **never**, as in the examples above:

1 I've never played bridge before.
2 It's the first time he's ever spoken to me.
3 It's the first time they've ever invited us to lunch.
4 We've never flown before.
5 It's the first time she's ever won a prize.
6 He's never written a novel before.
7 You've never complained about it before.
8 It's the first time I've ever asked you for money.
9 It's the first time we've ever had bad weather here.
10 She's never arrived late before.

65 Present Perfect/Past Simple

Compare these sentences:

My brother and his wife **have emigrated** to Australia.
They **left** on March 10th.

Notice that we use the Present Perfect when we do not specify what time in the past the action happened; **they have emigrated** means 'they emigrated some time recently and are still there'. We use the Past Simple when we are talking about a specific time in the past, e.g. **on March 10th**.

Read this conversation noticing the use of the tenses and then do the exercise below:

Every week Mr Pye, the manager of Leighton City Football Club, meets a reporter from the Leighton News *and gives him the latest news about the club. On August 28th, they had this conversation:*

Mr Pye Bad news! Fielding has broken his leg.

Reporter When did that happen?

Mr Pye Yesterday afternoon.

Reporter How did it happen?

Mr Pye He fell badly in a tackle.

We use the Present Perfect for the statement of fact at the beginning, but the Past Simple as soon as we ask questions about when, how, where, how much, etc.

Make short conversations between Mr Pye and the reporter on the same pattern as the one above, about the following news items. Ask questions with different appropriate questions words:

1 September 4th – City sold Bill Inwood to Rovers for £50,000.
2 September 11th – The City goalkeeper, Grant, was hurt in a car crash.
3 September 18th – City bought a new goalkeeper, James, from Leighton Town Football Club.
4 September 25th – James broke his ankle in a training match.
5 October 1st – Mr Pye won a prize as 'the unluckiest manager in the League'.
6 October 19th – City signed Johnny Briggs for £1,000,000.

66 Present Perfect with **for**, **since** with Past Simple

Compare these sentences:

We **haven't had** fish **for** a long time.
It's a long time **since** we **had** fish.

Rewrite these sentences, using the alternative form with **for** or **since**, as in the examples above:

1 It's a long time since we played tennis.
2 We haven't heard from her for a long time.
3 It's a long time since we had a party.
4 He hasn't written to me for a long time.
5 It's ages since her boy-friend took her out.
6 My wife hasn't rung me up at the office for ages.
7 It's years since he did any useful work.
8 It's six months since they paid us a visit.
9 You haven't bought me anything for ages.
10 It's a long time since I saw them.

67 Past Simple of **have** denoting experience

Look at these sentences:

We **had breakfast** early.
They **didn't have a good time** on holiday.

Here **have** refers to experience, not possession. When used in this way, **have** forms questions and negatives in the Past Simple with **did**.
When **have** refers to possession we can also use the form **had got**,
e.g.   I **didn't have** enough money to buy the dress.
       I **hadn't got** enough money to buy the dress.
Note that the **had got** form is never used to refer to experience.

Complete this dialogue, using the correct form of **have** (question or negative) a pronoun if necessary, and the appropriate noun. The first letter of each noun is given to help you.

e.g.   *A*   What _____ have for l_____?
        B   I _____ have l_____. I'm on a diet.
        A   What **did you** have for **lunch**?
        B   I **didn't** have **lunch**. I'm on a diet.

Toni   Hello, Jean. You've just come back from France, haven't you? ___1___ have a good h___1___?

Jean   Yes, We ___2___ have very good w___2___ at first but later it was quite sunny. The hotel was very pleasant.

Toni   ___3___ have all your m___3___ there?

Jean   Only breakfast. We ___4___ have l___4___ or d___4___ there because it was too expensive.

Toni   ___5___ have d___5___ at the hotel in the evenings?

Jean   Yes, on Saturday nights. But they ___6___ have good m___6___, and that was a pity, because I love dancing.

Toni   What else did you do in the evening?

Jean   Well, we went to the casino.

Toni   ___7___ have a good t___7___ there?

Jean   Yes, but we ___8___ have much l___8___. We lost all the time.

Toni   ___9___ have the o___9___ to meet any French people?

Jean   Yes, but I ___10___ have much c___10___ to speak French. They all spoke English.

Toni   And what about getting back? ___11___ have a good j___11___?

Jean   Well, we ___12___ have a very comfortable f___12___ but at least the air traffic controllers weren't on strike, as they usually are at this time of year.

68   Past Simple/Past Continuous

Notice the use of the tenses in these sentences:

When the phone **rang**, I **was painting** the bedroom ceiling.
When the phone **rang**, I **climbed down** the ladder to answer it.

Notice the use of the Past Continuous to indicate an action that was going on for some time, e.g. **I was painting**.

Match one item from List A and one from List B with each person on the left, and write two sentences about what he/she **was doing** and what he/she **did** afterwards:

> Last Thursday there was an explosion at a power station in London and the lights went out.

e.g. **When the lights went out, Alan was going to the newspaper office.**
When the lights went out, Alan interviewed the passers-by.

	A	**B**
Alan, journalist	1 reading a textbook	a stole a handbag as well
Barbara, nurse	2 waiting to go on stage	b closed the book and waited
Cora, actress	3 bathing the baby	c stood still because she was lost
Dagmar, tourist	4 serving drinks	d interviewed the passers-by
Eric, thief	5 going to the newspaper office	e told the children a story
Frank, student	6 taking a patient's temperature	f dropped a bottle of whisky
Gloria, mother	7 taking a wallet from a tourist	g sat down in her dressing room
Harry, barman	8 seeing the sights	h switched on the emergency power supply

69 Past Perfect Simple

a

Notice the verb forms used in these sentences:

> Mrs Fletcher **locked** the door and **went** to bed.
> When her husband **came** home, he **found** she **had locked** the door and **had gone** to bed.

We use the Past Perfect tense (**had** + Past Participle) when we want to talk about something that had happened before the main action in the past.

Use the Past Perfect to complete these sentences:

1 While Ida was answering the phone, the soup boiled over and the gas went out.
   When Ida got back to the kitchen, she found the soup _____.
2 While Harry was in the shop, someone stole his car.
   When Harry came out of the shop, he found that someone _____.
3 Moira left the front door open when she went to get the car out of the garage. While she was in the garage, the cat got out and climbed onto the roof.

When Moira came out of the garage, she found the cat _____.

4   Horace took Ellen to the cinema, but left her in the queue while he went to buy some cigarettes. While he was away, Marvin turned up and took Ellen into the cinema to see the film.

When Horace returned, he found that Marvin _____.

b   with **because**

Compare these sentences:

He played football for two hours in the morning and felt very tired in the afternoon.

He **felt** very tired in the afternoon because he **had played** football for two hours in the morning.

Rewrite these sentences, using the alternative form with **because** and the Past Perfect, as in the example above:

1   He won the match and celebrated his victory with his friends.
2   She didn't sleep much on the plane so she went to bed early that night.
3   He was bitten by a snake and had to go to hospital.
4   They left the door unlocked and a thief got into the house.
5   He didn't do all the questions so he failed the exam.

70   Second Conditional, **could, might**

Notice the verb forms used in these sentences:

A   If I **were (was)** rich, I **wouldn't work**. I**'d live** in a castle.
B   If you **lived** in a castle, you**'d be** lonely.
A   No, I **wouldn't**. If I **lived** in a castle, I **could have** a lot of servants and I **could invite** all my friends.
B   **Would you invite** me? (if you lived in a castle)
A   Well, I **might**. (invite you if I lived in a castle)

Note that **could** is used here to mean **would be able to**. **Might** is used to mean **perhaps . . . would**.

Complete the dialogue with the correct forms of the verbs in brackets. Use **could** and **might** where appropriate:

A   I wish I lived on a desert island, like Robinson Crusoe. If I __1__ (live) on a desert island, I __2__ (go) to the beach every day. I __3__ (lie) on the beach and __4__ (swim) when I felt like it.
B   What __5__ you eat? __6__ (not be) hungry?
A   Oh, I __7__ (pick) bananas from the trees, and if I __8__ (make) a fishing rod, I __9__ (catch) fish.

B But if you __10__ (want) to catch fish, you __11__ (need) a boat. You __12__ (have to) build one. And there __13__ (be) sharks in the water. It __14__ (be) dangerous.

A Oh, I __15__ (not worry) about them. I __16__ (keep) a look-out for them.

B But the biggest problem __17__ (be) water. What __18__ you (drink)?

A Oh, that __19__ (be) all right. There __20__ (be) a stream on the island.

B There __21__ (not be). Some islands haven't got streams.

A My island __22__ (have) a stream. If it __23__ (not have) one I __24__ (not go) there.

71 **wish** with Past Simple

Look at the passage below and notice the verb forms used after **wish**:

> David is a lonely little boy in a big city. He would like his life to be different. He would like to be able to do things he cannot do. He says, **'I wish we lived** at the seaside. **I wish I could go** swimming every day.'

a Change these statements into David's wishes, beginning **I wish**:

e.g.   He would like to be able to go horse-riding.
  I wish I could go horse-riding.

1 He would like to have a puppy.
2 He would like to be able to go to school on his bicycle.
3 He would like to be sixteen.
4 He would like to be able to play football every day.
5 He would like to work in a zoo.

b Change these statements into David's wishes, as in the example below:

e.g.   He would like to be able to go horse-riding. He would learn how to jump gates and hedges.
  I wish I could go horse-riding. If I could go horse-riding I'd learn how to jump gates and hedges.

1 He would like to have a puppy. He would take it to the park and play with it.
2 He would like to be sixteen. He would leave home and join the navy.
3 He would like to work in a zoo. He would look after animals.
4 He would like to have a boat. He would sail round the world.
5 He would like to live in the jungle. Then he would swing from tree to tree, like Tarzan.

72   Third Conditional

Notice the verb forms in these sentences:

> If he **had done** better in his exams, he **would have become** a doctor.
> In fact, he's now a very successful businessman.

Read this story:

> The other day I was talking to my friend Bernard. He teaches English in Spain. I asked him how he became an English teacher. He said:
>
> It's a long story. If a number of things in my life had been different, I wouldn't have come here and I wouldn't have become an English teacher.
>
> When I was at school, I wanted to become a pilot in the Air Force but my eyesight wasn't good enough. So I went to university and studied physics. I wanted to stay at university and do research. But my degree wasn't good enough. So I got a job with an engineering company.
>
> I liked the job and I expected to stay there for a long time, but then they appointed a new managing director. I didn't get on with him, so I applied for another job.
>
> I would probably have got the job, but on my way to the interview I met an old friend who worked in a travel agency. He offered me a job in Spain and I accepted it because I've always liked Spain.
>
> After two years, the agency wanted to send me to Greece, but then I met my wife, so I stayed. We got married but I didn't earn enough money to keep a family so I started giving English lessons at a school. The owner of the school wanted to retire so he offered me a full-time job as Director. I liked teaching more than working at the travel agency, so I took it. And that's how I became an English teacher.

Using the information in the story, say how Bernard's life might have been different, as in the example below:

> e.g. **If he had had good eyesight, he would have become a pilot in the Air Force.**

How would Bernard's life have been different?

1   if he had had good eyesight?
2   if his university degree had been better?
3   if the engineering company hadn't appointed a new managing director?
4   if Bernard had got on with him?
5   if he hadn't met his friend from the travel agency?
6   if he hadn't liked Spain?
7   if he hadn't met his wife?
8   if he had earned more money in the agency?
9   if the owner of the school hadn't wanted to retire?
10   if he hadn't liked teaching more than working at the travel agency?

73 Conditional Perfect (without **if** clause)

Look at these sentences:

A Why didn't you ring us up?

B I **would have done**, but I had forgotten your number. (I **would have done**, if I hadn't forgotten . . .)

We enjoyed our holiday very much and **would have liked** to stay there longer. (But I had to get back to work, we couldn't afford it, etc.)

The Conditional clause with **if** is understood, but not stated.
Note that in all cases the use of the Conditional Perfect tense automatically means that whatever is mentioned did not take place, i.e. **I didn't ring them up** in the first example, and **we didn't stay longer** in the second example.

Complete these sentences, using the verbs in brackets in the Conditional Perfect tense:

e.g.   I didn't know you were in hospital or I (visit) you.
      I didn't know you were in hospital or I **would have visited** you.

1 I (write) to you before now, but I have had so much work to do that I haven't had time.

2 It was such a beautiful place that she (like) to stay there for ever.

3 A What did you drink with the meal?
   B Beer. I (prefer) wine, but it was too expensive.

4 A Why didn't you tell me you were coming? I (meet) you at the station.
   B It (be) too much trouble.
   A Of course it wouldn't. I (not mind). I had nothing else to do.
   B Oh, well, I (not ask) you, anyway. I wanted my visit to be a surprise.

74 Alternatives to the Imperative

Notice how we can say the same thing more politely:

Get me a sandwich.
Get me a sandwich, **will you**?
Will you get me a sandwich, please.
Would you mind getting me a sandwich?

Look at these passages. Change the verbs in the Imperative to the alternative form given in the example at the beginning of each passage:

a *Colin Hammond is a very busy man, and is rather rude when his wife rings him at the office. He doesn't have time to talk to her. He says:*

e.g. **Ring me back later, will you?**

There are a few things I must tell you, though. I didn't have time to pay the gas bill. *Go round and pay it.* And I won't be able to play tennis with

Jack Frost this evening. *Ring him and tell him I can't play.*
Oh, yes, and *take the dog for a walk.* And *have a look at Brian's homework.*
And I'll be home late to dinner, so *leave it in the oven.*

b *He is a little more polite with his secretary. In the same situation, he says to her:*
    e.g. **Will you ring me back later, please.**

I've got to go out and see a customer. *Book a table at the Ritz.* And don't forget that I'm going to Birmingham tomorrow. *Find out the times of the trains.* And we must send out those letters this evening. *Type them before you go.* Oh, yes, and I can't see Mr Brown tomorrow. *Cancel my appointment with him.* And another thing – *ring my wife and tell her I'll be late home.*

c *He is more polite with his colleagues. In the same situation he says:*
    e.g. **Would you mind ringing me back later?**

I'm afraid I can't see you this morning. *Come up this afternoon.* I haven't had time to read the report you wrote. *Bring it with you.* And *make a note of the main points.* I need a list of last month's sales figures for the board meeting tomorrow. *Get it for me.* And I'll be at the board meeting all morning, so *deal with everything while I'm away.*

75   Imperative and **Why (not) do this?/Why do (don't) you do this?**

Compare B's responses each time:

    A   He does what he likes. He doesn't take any notice of what I say.
    B   **Why argue** with him, then?
        Why do you argue with him, then?
        Don't argue with him, then.

    A   We haven't had fish for some time.
    B   Then **why not have** fish?
        Then **why don't we have** fish?
        Get some fish, then.

For each response of B, give two alternative forms, as in the examples above:

    1   *A*   He always criticises my work and it upsets me.
        B   Why take any notice, then?
    2   *A*   I know smoking's bad for me.
        B   Why do you smoke, then?
    3   *A*   That programme always irritates me.
        B   Then don't watch it.
    4   *A*   I don't think I'm going to enjoy my holiday.
        B   Why are you going, then?
    5   *A*   They've done the job so badly it will have to be done again.
        B   Why are you going to pay them, then?

6   *A*   I've been working very hard and I feel tired.

      B   Then why don't you have a rest?

7   *A*   I feel very lonely.

      B   Come round to my house, then.

8   *A*   I'm sure I've been asked to pay too much income tax.

      B   Why not write to the tax inspector and complain, then?

9   *A*   I haven't seen her for ages. I wonder how she is.

      B   Ring her up, then.

10 *A*   I've got a headache.

      B   Then why not take an aspirin?

76 **Don't . . .** and **Be careful not to . . .**

Compare these sentences:

Be careful! **Don't take** any risks!

Be careful **not to take** any risks.

The only advice I can give is: **Don't bet** on horses!

The only advice I can give you is **not to bet** on horses.

Rewrite these sentences, using the alternative form, as in the examples above:

1   Take care! Don't lose the money!

2   The most important thing to remember in this situation is: Don't panic!

3   I warn you. Don't do that again!

4   Under the circumstances, the best advice I can give you is not to pay any attention to them.

5   The wisest course of action is: Don't give them any opportunity to complain!

Gerunds and infinitives

77 Verb + gerund, verb + infinitive

a Verb + gerund

Look at this sentence:

I **enjoy working** here.

Enjoy is followed by a gerund. Other verbs that always take a gerund are: **avoid, dislike, finish, (can't) help, (not) mind, practise, (can't) stand.**

Use one of these verbs to complete each of the following sentences. Do not use any verb more than once:

1 People wear safety belts to _____ being injured in accidents.
2 Would you _____ opening the window? It's very hot in here.
3 I _____ listening to classical music but I can't _____ queueing for hours outside concert halls to get a ticket.
4 When I _____ writing this book, I'm going to have a long holiday.
5 My aunt is very lonely. I can't _____ feeling sorry for her. But she _____ people visiting her without a good reason.
6 You must _____ answering this kind of question for the examination.

b Verb + preposition + gerund

Look at these sentences:

He **went on working** till he was seventy.
He's **got accustomed to living** in a cold country.

All verbs followed by a preposition (e.g. **on, to**) take a gerund.
Note that these verbs are followed by the preposition **to** and a gerund or noun phrase, not an infinitive:
amount to, be/get accustomed to, be given to, be opposed to, be/get used to, come near to, limit oneself to, look forward to, object to, resign oneself to.

Use one of these verbs to complete each of the following sentences. Do not use any verb more than once:

1 *A* We'll have to get up at six o'clock tomorrow.
   B That's all right. I'm _____ to getting up early.
2 I _____ to seeing you at the party on Saturday.
3 I _____ to paying taxes when I don't know where the money will go
4 He wanted to be a great solo violinist but he has realised that he isn't quite good enough, so he has _____ himself to playing in an orchestra.
5 If you make excuses that are obviously not true, it _____ to saying that you don't want to come.

c   Verb + infinitive without **to**
Look at these sentences:

> I **made him do** his homework.
> We **let them make** as much noise as they want.
> **Help me (to) carry** this.
> You **must try** harder.
> I'd **rather go** by car than walk.

Let and **make** take the infinitive without **to**. (See Practice 80.)
Help can be used with or without **to**.
Most auxiliaries such as **can, must, would**, etc. and **had better, would rather** (see Practices 56 and 58) take the infinitive without **to**.
Used denoting past habit takes an infinitive with **to**, e.g. **I used to go to school in London**. Compare **be used to**, **get used to**, which take the gerund. (See Section **b** above)

d   Verb + gerund or infinitive with **to**

A number of verbs can take a gerund or an infinitive with **to**. In many cases the meaning changes depending on whether a gerund or an infinitive follows the verb.Here is a list of the most common verbs of this type:

allow   The doctor doesn't **allow me to smoke**.
            We don't **allow smoking** in the classroom.
Allow takes an infinitive with an object, e.g. **me**; a gerund where there is none.

begin and   I'm **beginning/starting to feel** tired.
start   I **began/started smoking** when I was fourteen.
Begin and **start** take either an infinitive or a gerund. They are not normally found with a gerund in Continuous tenses, e.g. **I'm beginning**.

continue   I **continued to write** to him.
            I **continued writing** to him.
hate   I **hate living** in London.
            I'd **hate to live** on a boat.
In the Conditional form **hate** takes the infinitive, but the gerund is the usual form.

            I **hate to interrupt** you when you're working.
When the meaning is, as here, 'I'm sorry to interrupt you', **hate** takes the infinitive.

intend   I **intend to visit** them.
            I **intend visiting** them.
like   I **like to dance**.
            I **like dancing**.
Both forms can be used, but the gerund is slightly more usual when we are speaking generally to mean 'enjoy' or 'find agreeable'.

I **don't like waiting** on railway stations.
In the negative, when the meaning is the same as **dislike** the gerund is more common than the infinitive.

I **don't like to disturb** you.
When the meaning is, as here, 'I'm sorry to disturb you', **don't like** takes the infinitive. (Compare **hate**, above.)

I**'d like to help** you.
In the Conditional, **like** takes the infinitive.

love   I **love to walk**.
          I **love walking**.
The uses of **love** are the same as those of **like**.

prefer   I **prefer driving** to **walking**.
         I **prefer to drive** rather than **to walk**.
Prefer can take a gerund or an infinitive, but the gerund form is much easier to use and more idiomatic.

I**'d prefer to go** fishing.
The infinitive is used when **prefer** is in the Conditional; the reference here is to a particular preference on a certain occasion. In this sense we often use **would rather**. (See Section **c** above and Practice 58.)

remember I **remember/haven't forgotten smoking** my first cigarette.
and
forget   I **remembered/didn't forget to post** the letter.
Remember with a gerund means 'have the memory of', after the event; **remember** with the infinitive means 'not to forget', before or at the time of the event.
(**Remind** means 'make someone remember' and takes the infinitive, so **remind me to . . .** means 'don't let me forget to . . .', e.g. **Remind me to post the letter.**)

stop   He **stopped talking**. (He was silent.)
        He **stopped** (in the street) **to talk** to a friend.
Here both gerund and infinitive can be used, but with very different meanings. The first sentence means 'He was silent'. The second sentence means 'He stopped walking because he wanted to talk to his friend'.

try	I **tried to understand** it. (I made the effort, and perhaps I understood it, perhaps I didn't.)
	I **tried smoking** a cigarette for the first time. (I experimented to see if I would like it, and I actually smoked it.)

Use the correct forms of the verbs in brackets to complete these sentences. If you think both gerund and infinitive forms are possible, write both forms:

1 We don't allow (smoke) in the cinema.
2 We don't allow people (smoke) in the cinema.
3 He began (walk) slowly along the road.
4 I'm beginning (understand) how this works.
5 He continues (behave) in exactly the same way as he did when he was the manager.
6 I hate (play) rugby.
7 I'd hate (be) a teacher at that school.
8 I like (listen) to Mozart's music.
9 I like (read) the paper on the way to work in the mornings.
10 I'd like to (play) tennis tomorrow.
11 I don't like (stay) in bed late.
12 She preferred (play) tennis to (play) hockey.
13 I'd rather (play) tennis than hockey.
14 I remember (go) to the opera for the first time when I was ten.
15 Did you remember (book) the tickets for the opera?
16 She never stops (talk). I wouldn't like (be) her husband.
17 We stopped at the garage (get) some petrol.
18 I've tried (give up) smoking several times but I've never succeeded.
19 Why don't you try (smoke) a pipe? It would be better for you.
20 I forgot (include) 'forget' in this exercise, but then my co-author reminded me (put) it in.

78 Verbs of the senses + infinitive or **-ing**

Compare these sentences:

I **saw** the bomb **fall**.
I **watched** the rain **falling**.

We use the infinitive without **to**, e.g. **fall**, for a completed action; we use the participle, e.g. **falling**, for an incomplete or continuing action. The word order is the same in both cases.

Choose the more appropriate form for the verbs in brackets in this story:

There was a fire in our street yesterday morning. I woke up early. I pulled the curtains and suddenly saw smoke (1. pour) out of the house opposite. Then I heard the fire engines (2. ring) their bells and saw the first one (3. turn) the corner and (4. stop) outside the burning house. Then I saw a woman (5. stand) at the upstairs window. I watched her (6. open) the window and could see her (7. wave) at the firemen. I opened my bedroom window. Now I could hear more fire engines (8. arrive) and smell the smoke (9. come) from the burning house. Then I saw the firemen (10. carry) a large blanket into the front garden and (11. get) ready to catch the woman. Then I heard the chief fireman (12. shout) 'Jump'. For a long time, I watched the woman (13. hesitate) and the firemen (14. wait) underneath, (15. hold) the blanket. Then, suddenly, she made up her mind and I saw her (16. jump) safely into the blanket and heard the firemen and the neighbours (17. shout) 'Hurray'.

79 Preposition + gerund

Look at this sentence:

He's very **interested in gardening**.

The verb form after a preposition is always the gerund. The only exceptions are **but** and **except**,

e.g.   There's nothing we can do **but/except wait**.

Complete these sentences with an appropriate verb from the list in the **-ing** form: **do, drive, leave, live, lose, play, sit, speak, spend, use**. Use each verb once only.

1   Before _____ the office, there's something I'd like you to do for me.
2   They didn't say a word. They just sat in the corner without _____.
3   He's very fond of _____ the piano.
4   He returned to England after _____ several years abroad.
5   I'm a good driver but I wouldn't be capable of _____ a racing car.
6   I like this town. I've never thought of _____ anywhere else.
7   Why don't you do something, instead of _____ there in the armchair?
8   He solved the problem by _____ a different method.
9   I must put this money away in a safe place. I'm afraid of _____ it.
10 My fee for _____ this job will be £10.

80 **make** and **let** + infinitive

Look at these sentences:

A   **Let them go**! They haven't done anything wrong.
B   Yes, they have. They've broken my window and I'm going to **make them pay** for the damage.

Make and **let** are the only verbs immediately followed by the infinitive without **to**, apart from auxiliaries (**will, may, could**, etc.), and **help**, which can be used with or without **to**.

Complete these sentences with an appropriate verb from the list: **behave, do, eat, go, read, stay, take, talk, wait, watch**. Use each verb once only.

1 A You shouldn't let Ian ___1___ so many sweets, and you let him ___2___ up too late, too. You should make him ___3___ to bed earlier. And another thing, you let him ___4___ too much television. You ought to make him ___5___ his homework. When I was young, my father made us ___6___ properly at the dinner table, too. He didn't let us ___7___ with our mouths full. And he made us ___8___ until everyone had finished before we left the table.

B Oh, Mother! You'll tell me next that I shouldn't let Bob ___9___ his newspaper at breakfast.

A No, you shouldn't. Your husband's just as bad as your son. You ought to make him ___10___ you shopping in the car on Saturday afternoons, instead of going to the football match, and . . .

81   Verb + object + infinitive

Look at these sentences:

A What do you **want me to do**?
B **I'd like you to help** me carry this box.

Here is a list of common verbs that are followed by an object and an infinitive with **to**:
advise, allow, ask, cause, expect, force, help, invite, leave, order, pay, teach, tell, want, warn, would like.

Write down what John Stewart wants his secretary to do, and what Anne would like Erika to do:

e.g. **John Stewart wants his secretary to type the letters he has dictated.**
Anne would like Erika to wash up all the glasses.

1 *John Stewart, a businessman, is going out to lunch with a customer. Before leaving the office, he asks his secretary, Miss Jones, to do a number of things.*
Come in, Miss Jones. I'm going out now but I want you to do a few things for me while I'm out. First, would you type the letters I've dictated. Sign them for me and put them in the post. Then make an appointment for me with Mr Adams for Wednesday morning. After that, would you book my flight to Paris for Thursday, please, and also find me a hotel in Paris for two nights. Oh, yes, and put off the board meeting until I return from

Paris. Telephone my wife, would you, and tell her I'll be late home. And before you go, could you please file the papers on my desk.

2 *Erika is helping Anne clear up after a party. Anne tells her what she can do.*
First, wash up all the glasses, and leave them on the draining board in the kitchen. Then wrap the sandwiches in greaseproof paper and put them in the fridge. Empty the ashtrays in the dustbin, would you, and put the empty bottles in those cardboard boxes next to it. Then take the unopened bottles to the cellar. Oh, yes, you could hoover the carpet and dust the furniture. And after that, you can help me move the furniture back into the dining room.

82 Question word + infinitive

Look at these sentences:

Tell me **how to do** it.
He doesn't know **where to go**.
I'm not sure **how much to ask** for it.

We use this construction instead of more complicated ones like:
Tell me how I should do it.
He doesn't know where he has to go.
I'm not sure how much I should ask for it.

In the following passage choose the appropriate question words (the first letter of each one is given to help you), and change the words in italics into an infinitive:

e.g. I don't know w_____ *I must* be there.
I don't know **when to be** there.

I was once travelling from Spain to Switzerland, but I missed my train at the French border. I didn't know w___1___ *I should* do or w___2___ *I should* ask for advice. I wasn't sure whether I should wait 12 hours for another direct train or try to find out h___3___ *I could* get to Geneva by a different route. Eventually a man at the station told me w___4___ train *I ought to* catch and w___5___ *I had to* go to catch it. Meanwhile my friend in Geneva didn't know w___6___ *he should* do, either, when my original train arrived without me. He wasn't sure whether he ought to stay at the station or not. He didn't know h___7___ *he could* get in touch with me. He finally decided to leave a message for me, telling me w___8___ *I had to* go to contact him and w___9___ telephone number *I could* ring.

33 Infinitive and gerund forms

Infinitive

Compare these sentences:

> Would you like **to mention your uncle** in your will? (active)
> Would you like **your uncle to be mentioned** in your will? (passive)

Rewrite these sentences, using the alternative form, as in the examples above:

1 They want to replace the manager.
2 I think we should tell everyone about it.
3 She would like them to invite her, too.

Gerund

Compare these sentences:

> There is nothing new in **growing grapes** in England. (active)
> There is nothing new in **grapes being grown** in England. (passive)

Rewrite these sentences, using the alternative form, as in the examples above:

1 I'm not responsible for giving the information to the press.
2 He had nothing to do with changing the plans.
3 I wasn't conscious of anyone following me.

34 Double object verbs

Direct object

Compare these sentences:

> **Someone gave** the money to John. (active)
> **The money was given** to John. (passive)

We prefer the Passive when we are not especially interested in the doer of the action (e.g. **someone**), but rather in the object (e.g. **the money**).

Rewrite these sentences in the Passive, as in the example above:

1 At the end of the lesson, someone reads a story to the children.
2 Someone sold the shop to a friend of mine.
3 They have to pay back the loan to the bank.

Indirect object

Compare these sentences:

> **Someone gave** John the money. (active)
> **John was given** the money. (passive)

When we are more interested in the person to whom the action was done, i.e. the indirect object of the Active sentence, we can begin the

Passive sentence with the indirect object (e.g. **John**).
Other verbs which can be used in this form are: **ask, leave** (in a will),
lend, **owe**, **pay**, **promise**, **send**, **show**.

Rewrite these sentences in the Passive, beginning with the indirect object, as in the example above:
  1 People often ask Roy questions about his work.
  2 Someone showed me how to do it.
  3 Nobody owed me any money.
  4 I think they pay Harry too much.
  5 They promised Sarah a rise.

c   Direct and indirect object
Compare these sentences:

John was given the money. (passive)
The money was given to John. (passive)

Both of these sentences are Passive. In the first sentence we are more
interested in **John**, and in the second sentence we are more concerned
with **the money**.

Rewrite the sections in italics in the following conversation. Change the subject of each sentence
from a person to a thing, as in the example above:

*Mr Matthews, the bank manager, is worried about a loan the bank made to a
young couple to buy a house.*

| Mr Matthews | I think *they were lent the money* without enough guarantee. After all, *they were given the down-payment* as a wedding present. They haven't got any money themselves. |
| *Assistant manager* | Oh, that's all right. *We've been paid the whole amount.* I was *shown the letter* yesterday. *We were sent the cheque* last week. Apparently, *they were left the entire sum* in someone's will. |

85 Causative: **have/get something done**

a   Intentional
Compare these sentences:

I **painted my house** last month.
I **had my house painted** last month.
I **got my house painted** last month.

The first sentence means that I did the work myself; the second and
third sentences mean that someone painted it for me.

Get something done suggests a little more effort than **have something
done**, such as making a journey. So we may say when we leave home:

I'm going to the photographer's to get my photograph taken, but when we arrive, we say: **I've come to have my photograph taken**.

The people in these sentences are all going to **get something done**. Write down what each person says to her husband/his wife before he/she leaves, using the words in brackets:

    e.g. Lucy is going to the hairdresser's. (cut and perm my hair)
          I'm going to the hairdresser's to get my hair cut and permed.
1 Paula is going to the dry-cleaner's. (clean this dress)
2 Harry is going to the barber's. (cut my hair)
3 Peter is going to the TV shop. (repair this TV set)
4 Margaret is going to the jeweller's. (repair this watch)

The people in these sentences have just arrived at a shop or similar place where they want to **have something done**. Write down what each person says, using the words in brackets:

    e.g. Betty is at the dressmaker's. (alter this skirt)
          I've come to have this skirt altered.
5 Anne is at the optician's. (test my eyes)
6 Bob is at the tailor's. (make me a suit)
7 Frank is at a typing agency. (type this report)
8 Sarah is at the post office. (register this parcel)

b Unintentional

Look at these sentences:

        I **had my watch stolen** last week.
        He **got his nose broken** in a fight.

The constructions with **have** and **get** can be used when things happen to us although we do not want them to happen or ask for them to be done. There is a slight difference in meaning: the construction with **have** suggests the person was quite innocent, and the construction with **get** suggests that the person was partly responsible for what happened to him.

Rewrite the following account from Colin's point of view, changing the phrases in italics to a construction with **have** when Colin was in no way responsible for what happened, and to a construction with **get** when he was partly responsible:

    e.g. **In the first five minutes of the game, I had my shirt torn . . .**

Colin went to play rugby against another club. They were very tough players.

In the first five minutes of the game, *someone tore his shirt*. When he was lying on the ground, *someone kicked his head*. Colin was very angry. He started a fight, but *someone broke his nose* and *knocked out two of his teeth*. He was taken to the changing rooms and found that *someone had taken his wallet*. 'What a terrible place!' he said. 'Well, I suppose nothing worse can happen now.' He was wrong. While he was in hospital, *someone stole his car*.

Reported speech

86 Direct and reported speech

Compare these sentences:

He said, 'I don't like onions.' (direct)
He said **he didn't like onions**. (reported)
She said, 'I visited my aunt yesterday.' (direct)
She said **that she had visited her aunt the day before**. (reported)

Notice that when we change direct speech to reported speech, expressions of time and place (e.g. **yesterday**) often change. The tense will change also if the verb introducing the reported speech is in the past tense (e.g. **said**). Use this list of rules for reference when you do the exercises below. (See also Practice 127 on **say** and **tell**, and Practice 108 on Reported questions.)

Tense changes

Direct	Reported
'I'm working very hard.'	He said he was working . . .
'I earn £100 a week.'	He said he earned . . .
'I'm going to change my job.'	He said he was going to . . .
'I'll finish it soon.'	He said he would finish it . . .
'I've never seen her before.'	He said he had never seen her . . .
'I didn't break it.'	He said he hadn't broken it.
'I can run faster than her.'	He said he could run faster . . .
'It may be too late.'	He said it might be . . .

Time and place changes

Direct	Reported
here	there
this	that
now	then
yesterday	the day before
tomorrow	the day after
last week	the week before
next week	the week after
ago	before

1   Read this report of a conversation and then write what Janet and Mary actually said:
e.g.   *Janet*   **I'm going to the cinema . . .**

Janet told Mary that she was going to the cinema that evening with her husband. He was taking her to see *Kramer versus Kramer*. They were going to have dinner after the show. She was afraid there might be a queue so they were going to get to the cinema in good time to make sure they got in. She said she was very fond of Dustin Hoffman. In her opinion, he was the best actor in the world. She told Mary that she would tell her all about the film when she saw her the day after. Mary hoped they would both enjoy the film.

2 Put this conversation into reported speech:

e.g. **Mary said they were going on holiday the week after . . .**

Mary We're going on holiday next week. Ian and the children are looking forward to it. We're going to drive to the west of England and rent a caravan. Ian needs a rest, but he doesn't mind driving, and once we get to the caravan site we'll just stay there for a fortnight and put our feet up. The children will have plenty to do on the beach. The only trouble is that we can't rely on the weather at this time of year, but we'll have to take a chance on it and hope everything will be all right.

Janet I hope you'll enjoy your holiday. I'll see you when you get back and you can tell me all about it.

3 Read this report of a conversation and then write what Janet and Mary actually said:

e.g. *Janet* **Jack and I had a terrible time . . .**

Janet said she and her husband had had a terrible time at the cinema the night before. They had arrived early and had stood in a queue for an hour. But there had been so many people there that they couldn't get in. She had never felt so disappointed in her life. So they had come home and watched an awful programme on the television with three silly detectives. She supposed some people might think they were funny, but she had never seen such rubbish. Her husband (Jack) had fallen asleep. Mary said she had seen the programme, too, but she had turned it off after ten minutes.

4 Put this conversation into reported speech:

e.g. **Mary said that the caravan holiday had been a disaster . . .**

Mary The caravan holiday was a disaster. First of all, the car broke down on the way, so we had to spend the night in a hotel. The caravan site was a long way from the beach, and Ian had to take the children there by car so he didn't get much of a rest. The caravan itself wasn't large enough for a family. I've never slept in such an uncomfortable place. Finally, it rained all the time during the second week.

Janet I'm sorry you had such bad luck.

87 Tense changes: Present Simple and Future

Notice the tense changes from direct to reported speech in these sentences:

John I'm sure everything will be all right.
John **was** sure everything **would be** all right.

Jim When the boss comes in, I'll ask him about it.
Jim decided that when the boss **came** in, he **would ask** him about it.

Sheila If you don't keep your eyes on the road, you'll have an accident.
Sheila was afraid that if he **didn't keep** his eyes on the road, he**'d have** an accident.

In reported speech the Present changes to the Past, and **will** changes to **would**.
Note that the same changes referred to in Practice 86 apply here, e.g. **may** changes to **might**, **can** to **could**, **will have to** to **would have to**, etc.

Change the following to reported speech. Change the tenses in the same way as in the examples. Try not to use **said** all the time:

e.g. **Lucy** I don't suppose he'll have any problems.
Lucy didn't suppose that he would have any problems.

e.g. **Simon** I'm very worried about my mother.
Simon was very worried about his mother.

1 *Doctor Andrews* I believe that the operation will be successful.
2 *Martin* I hope that we will meet again.
3 *Mr Grenfell* I'm afraid that if we don't deliver the goods on time, we'll lose the order.
4 *Linda* I've made up my mind. I won't accept the job unless they pay me my travelling expenses.
5 *Mrs Roberts* I'm sure that when you see the report you'll reach the same conclusion.

88 Reported imperatives

a **tell someone to do something**

Compare these sentences:

Carol **Don't buy** that red shirt, Roger. It doesn't suit you. **Buy** the white one.
Carol **told Roger not to buy** the red shirt because it didn't suit him. She **told him to buy** the white one.

Notice how the infinitive with **to** is used in reported commands.

Change the following to reported speech:

The next day Carol was driving a car and Roger was giving her some advice.
1 Follow the main road as far as the traffic lights.
2 Slow down at the zebra crossing.
3 Look in the mirror.
4 Don't drive so fast.
5 Be careful of that cyclist. (Use **a**.)
6 Don't overtake that bus. (Use **a**.)
7 Turn left at the traffic lights.
8 Don't turn right.

b **ask someone to do something**

Compare these sentences:

Mr Crump   Students, will you listen to me, please.
Mr Crump **asked the students to listen** to him.
Mr Crump   Please don't smoke in the classroom, Alexander.
He **asked Alexander not to smoke** in the classroom.

Notice that a polite request with **please** is usually introduced by **ask** in reported speech.

Change the following to reported speech:

Mr Crump was giving his students some work to do in class.
1 Will you open your books, please.
2 Will you turn to page 37.
3 Please don't interrupt, Charlotte.
4 Will you do exercise 53, please.
5 Would you mind not talking, Alexander. (Do not use **mind**.)
6 Hand your books to me when you have finished, please.

89 either . . . or, neither . . . nor

a either . . . or

Read this dialogue noticing the use of **either . . . or**:

> *Harry* I know I need official permission to build a garage in my garden, but I don't know who to ask.
>
> *Paul* Ask the Town Council. They'll know. If they don't know, the Ministry of Town and Country Planning will know. Ask **either** the Town Council **or** the Ministry of Town and Country Planning.

Make two sentences using **either . . . or** for each of the following:

> e.g. Borg is through to the final of the tennis tournament.
> The two men in the semi-final are Connors and McEnroe.
> Who will play Borg in the final? Who will Borg play in the final?
> **Either Connors or McEnroe will play Borg.**
> **Borg will play either Connors or McEnroe.**

1 Mr Pye isn't sure who will play for Leighton City Football Club tomorrow, Allan or Bennett. Who is going to play? Who is Mr Pye going to choose?

2 Richard is going to get married. He has two close friends, Mark and Lawrence. Who's going to be the best man? Who is he going to ask?

3 One of the employees in Mr Carter's firm has stolen some money. He thinks it might be Harris, or perhaps Morley. Who does he suspect? Who does he think is responsible for the theft?

4 Happy Jack and Mountain Rose are favourites for the next race. Which horses do people think will win the race? Which horses are they going to bet on?

b neither . . . nor

Notice the use of **neither . . . nor**, **either**, **neither** and **nor** in these sentences:

> The Town Council **didn't know** the answer to Harry's question.
> The Ministry **didn't know, either.** (Neither/nor did the Ministry.)
> **Neither** the Town Council **nor** the Ministry **knew** the answer to Harry' question.

Rewrite each of the following statements twice, using two alternative forms, as in the example above:

1 Connors didn't win the tennis tournament. McEnroe didn't, either. Borg won it.

2 Allan didn't play in the match. Nor did Bennett. In the end, the manager chose Johnny Briggs.

3 Neither Mark nor Lawrence was best man at the wedding. Richard did not want to upset either of them, so Sally's brother was best man.

4 Harris didn't steal the money. Morley didn't, either. The thief was Mr Carter's nephew.

5 Happy Jack didn't win the race. Nor did Mountain Rose. The winner was London Pride.

90 although, even though, in spite of; however, nevertheless, all the same

Compare these sentences:

Although he was tired, he went on working.
Even though he was tired, he went on working.

In spite of being tired, he went on working.
In spite of his tiredness, he went on working.

He felt tired. **However,** he went on working.
He felt tired. **Nevertheless,** he went on working.
He felt tired. **All the same,** he went on working.

Although is followed by a subject and verb, **in spite of** by a gerund or a noun.
If we use **however, nevertheless** or **all the same,** two sentences are necessary.
All three could come at the end of the sentence,
e.g. **He went on working, however.**
We usually prefer to use a less formal construction, with **though,**
e.g. **He went on working, though.**

1 Rewrite the sentences with **although** into sentences using **in spite of,** and vice versa.
Use an appropriate noun after **in spite of** if you know one; if not, use a gerund form:

1 In spite of being an experienced driver, he drove carelessly.
2 Although he was strong, he could not break down the door.
3 In spite of being able to speak several languages, he's a terrible teacher. (Use **can.**)
4 Although they protest, the Government won't do anything.
5 Although she was very distressed, she smiled bravely.
6 In spite of his laziness, he is very intelligent.
7 In spite of her rudeness, I still like her.
8 In spite of his wealth, he still lives in that old house.
9 Although he played well, he lost the game.
10 The plane took off on time, although it was foggy.

2 Rewrite the above, using two sentences with **though** at the end of the second sentence:
e.g. **He was an experienced driver. He drove carelessly, though.**

91 Future time clauses with **as soon as, when, before**

Notice the tenses of the verbs in these sentences:

I'll telephone him **as soon as I get** home.
When you see Fred, tell him I want to see him.
They'll get everything ready **before she arrives**.

Notice that the verb after **as soon as**, **when** and **before** is in the Present Simple tense.

Use an appropriate verb in the Present Simple in each space to complete the dialogue:

Mr Gray   Is Mr Hall there?

Anne   No, I'm afraid he's gone out.

Mr Gray   Well, as soon as he ___1___ back, will you ask him to ring me, please? No, I've got a better idea. I'm expecting an important customer and when he ___2___, I'll have to take him out to lunch. So, when you ___3___ Mr Hall, will you give him this message? I've left a report for him on his table. I want him to read it as soon as he ___4___ in. When he ___5___ it, he'll see that it's important. I want him to give me his opinion as soon as I ___6___ back to the office after lunch.

Anne   All right, Mr Gray, I'll tell Mr Hall when he ___7___. Will you ring him when you ___8___ ready to see him?

Mr Gray   Yes, as soon as I ___9___ free. But tell him he must make up his mind about the report before I ___10___ him.

92 Infinitive of Purpose

Compare these answers:

A   Why did you go out into the garden?
B   **Because I wanted to get** some fresh air.
     To get some fresh air.

Replace the words in italics in this dialogue with the infinitive:

e.g.   I have to get up at 6.00 **to catch** the 7.00 train.

Mark   Hello, Brian. How are you? I haven't seen you for ages.

Brian   No. We moved to the country six months ago.

Mark   How are you getting on? Do you like it?

Brian   No. We're fed up with it. I spend all day travelling. I have to get up at 6.00. *I have to catch* the 7.00 train. My wife needs the car.
(1) *She has to take* the children to school. At first we sent them to the village school. (2) *We wanted to avoid* that problem. I took the

car to London. (3) *I hoped to save* money. But Jane, my daughter, wanted to go to a school in Harford (4) *because she wanted to study* music, and Harry, my son, went there, too, (5) *because he wanted to do* Spanish, and the council isn't going to start a bus service (6) *that will take* two children to school.

Mark   Why did you move to the country?

Brian   (7) *Because we wanted to escape* from the noise and smoke. But now a company is building a factory near us. (8) *They intend to provide* work for people in the village. I just can't win!

93   so as to, in order to, so that, because; avoid, prevent

a   to, so as to, in order to, so that, because

Compare these sentences:

He changed his job **to be** free to referee football matches.
He changed his job **so as to be** free to referee football matches.
He changed his job **in order to be** free to referee football matches.
He changed his job **so that he would be** free to referee football matches.
He changed his job **because he wanted to be** free to referee football matches.

All are acceptable English. However, we normally use **to** in simple statements,

e.g.   **He went to the station to meet his friend.**

We use **so as to** and **in order to** in more formal circumstances; the **in order to/so as to** clause usually comes first.

e.g.   **In order to/So as to deal with the growing problem of unemployment, we have set up a number of Employment Centres in the city.**

So that or **because** are essential when there is a change of subject,

e.g.   **We have set up Employment Centres so that people will know where to go for advice.**
   We have set up Employment Centres because we want people to know where to go for advice.

Use **so as to** or **in order to** instead of **because/if** in the following sentences. Put the clause with **in order to** or **so as to** first:

e.g.   They are building a lot of hotels because they want to develop their tourist trade.
   In order to develop their tourist trade they are building a lot of hotels.

1   The Ministry has published a road safety booklet because it wants to inform people about changes in the Highway Code.

2   We have designed training courses because we want to improve the standard of hotel management.

3 We have opened a number of branch offices because we want to provide a better service to our customers.

4 He employed a different method because he wanted to test his findings.

5 Please hand your passport application to this office a month before you intend to travel abroad if you want to avoid delay.

b **so as not to, in order not to, so that . . . not, to avoid, because . . . not**

Compare these sentences:

He came in quietly **in order not to wake** the baby.

He came in quietly **so as not to wake** the baby.

He came in quietly **so that he would not wake** the baby.

He came in quietly **to avoid waking** the baby.

He came in quietly **because he didn't want to wake** the baby.

Note that the simple infinitive with **to** is not possible with the negative.

Rewrite each sentence in two ways, using **in order not to, so as not to, so that . . . not** or **to avoid**:

e.g. Check everything you write, so as not to make silly mistakes.
Check everything you write, to avoid making silly mistakes.
Check everything you write, so that you don't make silly mistakes.

1 If you work in a chemical laboratory, you should wear gloves so that you will not expose your skin to harmful substances.

2 Some dentists wear masks so as not to catch germs from their patients.

3 The thief wore gloves to avoid leaving fingerprints.

4 He put his keys on a key-ring so as not to lose them.

5 We process all the waste products from the factory so that we won't pollute the river.

c **so that . . . not, to prevent, because . . . not**

Compare the following sentences:

The cinema has two exits **so that people will not be trapped** inside.

The cinema has two exits **to prevent people from being trapped** inside.

The cinema has two exits **because we don't want people to be trapped** inside.

Rewrite each sentence in two ways, using **so that . . . not**, and **to prevent** instead of **because . . . not**, as in the examples above:

1 We are doing research because we don't want our competitors to gain an advantage over us.

2 We tell women who work in the factory to wear hairnets because we don't want their hair to be caught in the machines.

3 He cleaned the bicycle carefully because he didn't want it to get rusty.

4 They have put broken glass on top of the walls because they don't want thieves to get in.

5 *The Samaritans* provide lonely people with telephone numbers to ring when they are depressed because they don't want them to commit suicide.

4 Defining relative clauses

Notice the relative pronouns in these sentences:

The man **who/that** took my bag was tall, with a red beard.
The jewellery **which/that** was in the bag was my mother's.
The gun **which/that** he had wasn't loaded.

Read this story and use the information given to complete the exercises which follow:

Two weeks ago, two masked bandits, a man and a girl, raided the City Bank in Worsley. A third bandit was waiting for them outside in a stolen red Ford. At first the cashier refused to hand over the money in the safe. A customer tried to run away and the male bandit shot and wounded him. Then the cashier gave the bandits the money in a black suitcase. They escaped and a clerk rang the police. The police found the red Ford two miles away. A housewife said she had seen them abandon it and get into a black Talbot (registration number ABC 123R). The owner of the Ford rang up to report the theft. Three hours later a woman telephoned the police in Essex. She had been riding her horse along a country road near a farmhouse when a black Talbot had suddenly come round the corner very fast and frightened the horse. She had fallen off and rung to complain. Later, she had seen the car outside the farmhouse. The farm belonged to Mr John Holmes, but he was not there. The police telephoned the farm and a girl's voice answered. Inspector Sanders drove to the farmhouse with three policemen. They found the car, an empty black suitcase, a gun with one shot fired and a lighter with the initials B.C., and in different parts of the farmhouse there were the fingerprints of two known criminals, Alf Slade and Ernie King. Two hours later they were arrested at a cinema in a small town nearby; there was a girl with them, Bonnie Clyde. Slade admitted that he had robbed the bank, and King said that he had driven the getaway car. They refused to say where they had hidden the money. The farmer, Mr Holmes, found it when he was ploughing a field a few days later. He told the police he had rented the farm to a girl and then gone away on holiday.

Characters: Inspector Sanders (detective)
             Alf Slade, Ernie King and Bonnie Clyde (bank robbers)
             Percy Simpson (cashier)
             Anne Wilson (bank clerk)
             James Long (driver)

Jeremy Lake (customer)
Doris Baines (housewife)
John Holmes (farmer)
Cynthia Beaufort (horsewoman)

a **who/that**

He interviewed Alf Slade, because he was **the man who/that** robbed the bank.

Who is more commonly used for persons than **that**.

Write sentences, as in the example, for all the characters listed above, explaining why Inspector Sanders wanted to interview them.

b **which/that**

The red Ford was **the car that/which** was waiting outside the bank.

Which and **that** are used for things.

Complete these questions and answers, using a noun and a relative pronoun in each space:

1   A   Was the black Talbot _____ was found two miles from the bank?
    B   No, it was the red Ford which was found there.
2   A   Which clues proved the bandits guilty?
    B   The _____ had contained the money, the _____ had fired the shot at Mr Lake, the _____ had Bonnie Clyde's initials on it. They were all found in the farmhouse.

c **whose**

James Long was the man whose car was stolen.

Complete these sentences, using **whose**, as in the example above:

1   _____ farmhouse was rented.
2   _____ horse was frightened.
3   _____ initials were found on the lighter.
4   _____ fingerprints were found in the farmhouse.
5   _____ telephone call took the police to Essex.

d   Omission of object pronoun

The man (whom/that) **the bandits wounded** is now in hospital.
The money (that/which) **the bandits took** was found in a field.

In the first sentence it was the bandits who wounded the man; he didn' wound them. Similarly, in the second sentence the bandits took the money, not the other way round.
When the person or thing referred to in a defining relative clause is the object of the verb, not the subject, we usually omit the relative pronoun

Complete these sentences in the same way as the examples above. You must put an object (e.g. **man**) and a subject (e.g. **the bandits**) in each sentence. You can also use **whom**, **which** or **that**, but these are usually omitted:

1   The _____ held up at first refused to hand over the money.
2   The _____ shot was trying to run away.
3   The _____ raided was in Worsley.
4   The _____ drove away from the bank was a red Ford.
5   Who were the _____ interviewed at the bank?
6   The _____ saw were a red Ford and a black Talbot.
7   The _____ rented belonged to Mr Holmes.
8   The _____ found had the initials B.C. on it.
9   Who were the _____ arrested?
10   What were the _____ found in the farmhouse?

e   Relative pronoun as object of a preposition

The farmer (whom/that) **the bandits spoke to** went away on holiday.
The money (that/which) **the police were looking for** was found in a field.

When the person or thing referred to in a defining relative clause is the object of a verb with a preposition, we usually omit the relative pronoun.

Complete these sentences in the same way as the examples above. Put a subject (e.g. **the police**) in each sentence. You can also use **whom**, **which** or **that**, but these are usually omitted:

1   The masked bandits _____ was waiting for jumped into the car.
2   The money _____ handed over was put into a black suitcase.
3   The girl _____ talked to when they telephoned was Bonnie Clyde.

f   **where**

This is **the village I was born in.** (in which I was born)
This is **the village where I was born.**

When the preposition in a defining relative clause refers to the place, we usually prefer to use the relative adverb, **where**.

Rewrite these sentences, changing the section in italics to a form with **where**, as in the example above:

1   Compton Street, two miles from the bank, is *the street the bandits left the car in.*
2   This is *the road my horse was frightened in*, and that's *the farmhouse the bandits' car was found at.*
3   The Regal, not far from Mr Holmes's farmhouse, is *the cinema the bandits were arrested at.*
4   This is *the field the bandits hid the money in.*
5   This is the postcard of *the hotel Mr Holmes spent his holiday at.*

NOTE When the preposition refers to time, we usually prefer to use **when** in the same way,

e.g. **Six o'clock! That's the time the pubs open at. (at which the pubs open)**
Six o'clock! That's the time when the pubs open.

g **the way (in which)**

I didn't like **the way** (in which) **he did it.**
I didn't like **the way in which it was done.**

When a defining relative clause refers to the way in which something was done, we can either use **which** or omit it. When we use the passive (a more formal construction), we prefer to use **which**.

Change the relative clauses in these sentences to the passive and include **in which**, as in the example above:

1 There are several ways we could improve the company's products.
2 The programme is intended to show ways companies cheat the public.
3 The way they discovered the crime was very simple.
4 There are a number of ways they could change the system of taxation.

95 Non-defining relative clauses

Look at these sentences:

The police have been investigating a robbery at the City Bank. They have just announced that three people have been arrested.
The police, **who have been investigating a robbery at the City Bank,** have just announced that three people have been arrested.
In that cell you'll find Bonnie Clyde. **The police have just arrested her.**
In that cell you'll find Bonnie Clyde, **whom the police have just arrested.**

Notice that the clause with **who** does not define which people we are talking about, but gives us additional information about them. The information can also be given in a separate sentence.

1 Complete this story, using **who, whom, which, whose** or **where** in each space:

Two weeks ago, two masked bandits, __who__ have since been identified as Alf Slade, 32, and Bonnie Clyde, 23, raided the City Bank, __1__ local office at 31 High Street was also raided earlier this year. A third bandit, Ernie King, 29, was waiting outside in a red Ford, __2__ was later reported stolen by the owner. Mr Jeremy Lake, a customer, __3__ tried to escape, was shot and wounded. The cashier then handed over the money, __4__ the bandits put in a black suitcase. They then made their escape in the Ford, __5__ was later found abandoned two miles away. Mrs Doris Baines, __6__ lives at 59

Compton Street, Worsley, and __7__ house overlooked the place where the bandits had left a second car, __8__ was a black Talbot, registration number ABC 123R, saw them change cars.

Three hours later, a lady in Essex, Miss Cynthia Beaufort, __9__ was riding her horse along a country road, suddenly came face to face with the black Talbot, __10__ turned a corner and frightened her horse. Later she saw the car parked outside Ringwood Farm, __11__ belongs to Mr John Holmes, __12__ was on holiday in Mallorca at the time. The police, __13__ suspicions were aroused by the description of the car when Miss Beaufort telephoned to complain, rang the farmhouse, and the phone was answered by a girl, __14__ voice was recorded and played back to Mr Lake, __15__ she had told to lie down during the robbery.

Inspector Sanders of Scotland Yard, __16__ was accompanied by three policemen, drove to the farmhouse, __17__ he found the black Talbot car, an empty black suitcase, __18__ had been used to carry the money, a gun, __19__ had been fired once, and a lighter, __20__ had the initials B.C. on it. The police searched the farmhouse, __21__ they found fingerprints but no sign of the money, __22__ the bandits had apparently hidden. Two hours later the bandits were arrested at the Regal Cinema, Minton, __23__ they had been watching a film. Slade, __24__ admitted his part in the robbery, and King, __25__ had driven the getaway car, were arrested. Bonnie Clyde, __26__ only connection with the crime was the lighter and the record of her voice, denied robbing the bank with the others, __27__ she had only just met, according to her statement. But John Holmes, __28__ farm had been rented for two weeks while he was on holiday in Mallorca, identified her on his return as the girl who had rented it. A few days later, Mr Holmes, __29__ had been asked to come back to England for the inquiry, discovered the stolen money, __30__ had been buried in one of his fields.

Join these sentences together, using a relative clause and the pronoun given in brackets:

e.g.   The police have arrested Alf Slade, 32 and Ernie King, 29. They are accused of having robbed the City Bank. (who)

   The police have arrested Alf Slade, 32, and Ernie King, 29, who are accused of having robbed the City Bank.

1   The police arrested Alf Slade, 32, and Ernie King, 29, for the robbery at the City Bank. Slade and King have decided to plead guilty. (who)

2   The two men in this cell are Alf Slade and Ernie King. The police arrested them for the robbery at the City Bank. (whom)

3   A red Ford was found two miles from the bank. It was used by the bandits in the robbery. (which)

4   In the robbery, the bandits used a red Ford car. It was found two miles away. (which)

5 A red Ford car was found two miles from the bank. The bandits used it in the robbery. (which)
6 Two miles from the bank the police found a red Ford car. The bandits used it in the robbery. (which)
7 Cynthia Beaufort's horse was frightened by the bandits. She rang the police to complain. (whose)
8 The bandits frightened Cynthia Beaufort's horse. She rang the police to complain. (whose)
9 Mr Holmes's farm is in Essex. The bandits hid the money there. (where)
10 The police have been asking questions at the City Bank. The robbery took place there. (where)

96 Co-ordinating relative clauses

Compare the use of **which** in these sentences:

One of the bandits was waiting outside the bank in **a red Ford, which** was later reported stolen. (**Which** refers to the Ford.)
One of the bandits was waiting outside the bank in a red Ford, which shows they had planned the raid thoroughly. (**Which** refers to the fact that one of them was waiting outside in the car.)

The first sentence contains a non-defining clause introduced by **which**. The relative pronoun **which** refers only to **a red Ford**. Sentences like this can also use the pronouns **who** or **whom**.
The second sentence is of a different type; it contains a co-ordinating or connecting relative clause.
The relative pronoun **which** refers to the whole main clause, **one of the bandits was waiting outside the bank in a red Ford**. In sentences like this, the relative pronoun is always **which**.

Underline that part of each sentence to which the word **which** refers. Then make a question to which the section you have underlined is the answer:

e.g. a Miss Beaufort suddenly came face to face with a <u>black Talbot</u>, which turned the corner and frightened her horse.
b <u>Miss Beaufort suddenly came face to face with a black Talbot,</u> which proves that the bandits had already driven to Essex.
a **What turned the corner and frightened Miss Beaufort's horse?**
b **What proves that the bandits had already driven to Essex?**
1 a Mr Holmes discovered the stolen money, which pleased the bank.
b Mr Holmes discovered the stolen money, which had been buried in one of his fields.

2 a Salesmen offer to pay for improvements to people's houses, which can include such things as repairing the roof or even knocking down walls.

   b Salesmen offer to pay for improvements to people's houses, which means that the owner is under an obligation to them.

3 a People who are against fox-hunting often lay false trails for the hounds, which spoils the hunt.

   b People who are against fox-hunting often lay false trails for the hounds, which follow them and forget about the fox.

4 a Mars is apparently red because it is covered with iron oxide, which is reddish in colour.

   b Mars is apparently red because it is covered with iron oxide, which means that there must be oxygen in the soil there.

97 **there is/are** as alternatives

The constructions with **there is/there are** are usually more common than the alternative constructions. Note that the alternative constructions never begin with **it** or **they**.

a **Some food is left, there is some food left**

Compare the sentences on the left with those on the right, which use **there is/are**:

Some food is left.	There is some food left.
A little food is left.	There is a little food left.
Not much food is left.	There is not much food left.
A lot of food is left.	There is a lot of food left.
A great deal of food is left.	There is a great deal of food left.
A few people are outside.	There are a few people outside.
Several people are outside.	There are several people outside.
Twenty people are outside.	There are twenty people outside.
A lot of people are outside.	There are a lot of people outside.
Hundreds of people are outside.	There are hundreds of people outside.

Rewrite these sentences, using **there is/are**, **there was/were** or **there will be**:

1 Seventeen watches are in the suitcase.
2 Only a few people are in the audience.
3 In those days, not many cars were on the road.
4 Nothing in the law is against it.
5 A few biscuits are in the tin.
6 Thousands of people will be there.

b **there is/are** and **exist**

Compare these sentences:

There is often **bad feeling** between employers and employees.
Bad feeling often **exists** between employers and employees.

Rewrite these sentences, using the correct form of **there is/are**, as in the example above:

1 Evidence exists that he is guilty.
2 People like that have always existed.
3 No ghosts exist in this house.
4 Little satisfaction exists in winning games by cheating.
5 No proof that he had done it existed.

c **there is/are** and **have**

Compare these sentences:

The house has ten bedrooms. **There are** ten bedrooms in the house.
We should have a law against it. **There should be** a law against it.

Rewrite these sentences, using the correct form of **there is/are**, as in the examples above:

1 I've got several chairs and a sofa in my room.
2 We've got some whisky in the cupboard.

3 We haven't got enough wood to make a fire.
4 The village had a lot of strange customs.
5 I haven't anything important to tell you.
6 We'll have plenty of time to solve the problem.

d **there is/are** and **happen, take place, occur**

Compare these sentences:

An accident happened at the corner of the street yesterday.
There was an accident at the corner of the street yesterday.

A party will take place on Saturday night.
There will be a party on Saturday night.

In describing events, **there is/are** is often used instead of verbs like **happen, take place** or **occur**.

Rewrite these sentences, using the correct form of **there is/are**, as in the examples above:

1 A revolution took place in this country a few years ago.
2 A lot of accidents happen on this road.
3 Cases like this have occurred before.
4 Elections should take place every two years.
5 I don't think a war will occur.
6 If people behaved better, arguments like this would not occur.

e **there is/are** + relative clause

Compare these sentences:

Some people still believe the earth is flat.
There are still **some people who** believe the earth is flat.

I don't like many of my teachers at school, but I like **some of them**.
I don't like many of my teachers at school but **there are some (of them that)** I like.

In some cases, **there is/are** is used with a relative clause to make the meaning more emphatic.

Make the sentences below more emphatic, using **there is/are** in the same way as the examples above:

1 A few people do their own weather forecasts.
2 At the end of the American War of Independence, a number of people still wanted a king.
3 Most of our employees live near the factory but a few travel long distances every day.
4 I've answered most of the questions, but I can't do a few.
5 A man in our village makes models of ships.
6 Some people will do anything for money.
7 You can have most of these books. I don't want to keep many of them.
8 I must go to London next week. I have to see a number of people.

98   **its, it's, it is**

Note the spelling in these sentences:

The dog is looking for **its** master.
It's a lovely day.
The weather forecast said it would be a nice day today, and **it is**.

Note that we use the short form **it's**, instead of **it is**, in spoken English except at the end of the clause,
e.g. **She's tall.**
I'm taller than she is.

Complete this dialogue, using **its, it's** or **it is**:

Mother   __1__ time for the cat to have __2__ dinner. Put the milk in __3__ saucer.

Susan   I don't know where __4__.

Mother   __5__ in the cupboard in the kitchen where the plates are. At least, I think __6__. Have a look, and if __7__ not there, tell me.

Susan   I can't find it. Oh, yes, here __8__. Does the cat know __9__ dinner's ready?

Mother   Of course it does. __10__ always hungry.

9 Adverbs of frequency

Notice the position of the adverbs in these sentences:

A Are the girls **ever** late for class?

B Well, Susan is **always** late. Judy isn't **often** late, but she lives nearer.

A Have you **ever** been in a casino before?

B No, I've **never** been in one, but I've **always** wanted to play roulette.

A Have you **ever** been asked this question before?

B Well, no. I've **sometimes** been asked rude questions, but I've **never** been asked one as rude as that.

A Why do they **always** call their union meetings on Wednesdays? They know I **always** play golf on Wednesday afternoons.

B Yes, but they don't **usually** think about that when they arrange the meeting.

The frequency adverbs usually occur after the verb **be** and before other verbs,
e.g. **Susan is always late.**
   I always play golf.
When there is a compound verb, frequency adverbs usually appear between the auxiliary and the participle or verb stem,
e.g. **I've always wanted a horse.**
   They don't usually work late.

Use the adverbs in brackets at the end of each sentence to complete the dialogue below. Put the adverb in the most usual position:

Julie Will you love me? (always)

Roger Well, that's a difficult question to answer. (always) I've asked myself that. (often)

Julie Really? And do you get the same answer? (always)

Roger Yes, of course. But I've wondered about it, (sometimes) because marriages don't last (always) and things go wrong. (often) But I've been sure (always) that I could be happy without you. (never)

Julie How nice! Has it occurred to you that I might be happy without you? (ever)

Roger Oh! Well, I know I'm a bit selfish (sometimes) and I've been told (occasionally) that I don't pay enough attention to you, (always) but I look at other girls (never) and I remember your birthday (always) and . . . Could you imagine living without me? (ever)

Julie Well, I managed it for twenty years. I think you take me for granted. (sometimes) I don't say anything about it (usually) but I'll remember this conversation, (always) and if I ask you the same question again (ever) . . .

100 **enough, too**

Notice the position of **enough** and **too** in these sentences:

> I can't afford to buy the dress. I haven't got **enough money**.
> I haven't got **enough money** to buy the dress.
> I can't carry all those suitcases. I'm not **strong enough**.
> I'm not **strong enough** to lift all those suitcases.
> I'm **too weak** to lift all those suitcases.
> That horse will never win a race. It doesn't run **fast enough**.
> It will never run **fast enough** to win a race.
> That horse runs **too slowly** to win a race.

> **Enough** comes before a noun but after an adjective or adverb.
> **Too** always comes before an adjective or adverb.

a Make a sentence with **too** and a sentence with **not . . . enough** for each person, using the adjectives in brackets:

> *Harry Boyd runs an employment agency but he finds it difficult to get jobs for his clients.*
> e.g. Sally, typist (careless/careful)
> **Sally can't get a job as a typist. She's too careless.**
> **She's not careful enough.**
> 1 Olga, actress (ugly/pretty)
> 2 Fred, policeman (short/tall)
> 3 Annabel, model (fat/slim)
> 4 Horace, salesman (shy/aggressive)
> 5 Sid, waiter (rude/polite)

b Rewrite the sentences on this pattern:

> e.g. **Sally's too careless to get a job as a typist.**
> **Sally's not careful enough to get a job as a typist.**

c Explain why some more of Harry's clients can't get jobs. Make a sentence with **too** and a sentence with **not . . . enough** for each person, using the adverbs in brackets:

> e.g. Roddy, driving instructor (drives fast/carefully)
> **Roddy can't get a job as a driving instructor.**
> **He drives too fast. He doesn't drive carefully enough.**
> 1 Lavinia, secretary (dresses untidily/smartly)
> 2 Boris, English teacher (speaks quickly/clearly)
> 3 Bill, road mender (works slowly/hard)
> 4 Zeke, rock singer (sings softly/loudly)
> 5 Adam, political agent (thinks honestly/crookedly)

d Rewrite the sentences on this pattern:

> e.g. **Roddy drives too fast to get a job as a driving instructor.**
> **Roddy doesn't drive carefully enough to get a job as a driving instructor.**

01 Reported speech: exclamations

Notice the word order of these sentences:

How poor they were! (direct speech)
When I saw the villagers I realised **how poor they were**. (reported speech)

What awful weather (we had)! (direct speech)
You can't imagine **what awful weather we had**. (reported speech)

What a beautiful present (she gave me)! (direct speech)
You'd be surprised to see **what a beautiful present she gave me**. (reported speech)

Change these sentences from direct to reported speech in the same way as the examples above:

1 What a mess (they made)!
   You should have seen _____.
2 How tired I was!
   You'll hardly believe _____.
3 What a terrible accident (it was)!
   You can't imagine _____.
4 How pretty she looked!
   You should have seen _____.
5 How stupid some people are!
   It's amazing _____.
6 How dangerous it was!
   We didn't realise until afterwards _____.

02 Reported speech: questions

Look at the word order in these questions:

Where are they going? (direct question)
I wonder **where they are going**. (reported question)

How much does it cost? (direct question)
Ask him **how much it costs**. (reported question)

Did she go with him? (direct question)
I wonder **if she went with him**. (reported question)

Change the direct questions to reported questions, beginning with the words in brackets:

e.g. Does she want any tea? (Ask her)
    Ask her if she wants any tea.

1 Where does he live? (Tell me)
2 How much did you pay for it? (I'd like to know)
3 What is she going to do next? (I wonder)
4 What's the time? (Ask that policeman)
5 Does he always behave like that? (I wonder)

6   Did they win the game? (I wonder)
7   What do you think about your chances in the game? (Tell me)
8   How did they hear about it? (I wonder)
9   Is she coming to the party? (Ask her)
10 What will the weather be like tomorrow? (I wonder)
11 Which team does he play for? (Ask him)
12 Who did she speak to? (Ask her)
13 Who's the lucky man? (I wonder)
14 Why did you say that? (Tell me)
15 Who does she think she is? (Ask her)

103   Direct and Indirect object: **Explain it to me**

Look at this sentence:

I **explained** the situation **to him**.

A number of verbs take this construction:
verb + direct object + **to** + indirect object.
but not the alternative shown in Practice 104:
verb + indirect object + direct object.
The commonest verbs of this kind are:
announce, describe, entrust, explain, introduce, propose, suggest.

Complete these sentences, using an appropriate form of one of these verbs. Do not use any verb more than once:

1   I _____ him to my sister. She had never met him before.
2   At the end of the competition, she _____ the names of the winners to the public.
3   The radio commentator _____ the match to the listeners.
4   I wouldn't like to _____ the money to him. He's not reliable.
5   The customer was very angry at first, but when I _____ what had happened to him, he understood that it was not our fault.

104   Direct and Indirect object: **Give it to me**

Compare these sentences:

He **lent me** some money.
He **lent** some money **to me**.

The verb **lend** can have a direct object (e.g. **some money**) and an indirect object (e.g. **me, to me**). The sentences above show the two constructions in which it can be used.
The commonest verbs of this type are: **give, guarantee, leave (money), lend, make (an offer, a present), offer, owe, promise, read (a story), refuse (a loan), sell, send, show, teach (a language, etc.), tell (a story, write (a letter).**

A few verbs have special points to be noted:

buy   **He bought a present for his wife.**
             He bought her a present.

When a preposition is used with **buy**, it is **for**, not **to**.

ask   **I asked John a question.**
             I asked him his name.
             She asked me the way.

Ask is not used with **to**.

ask for **I asked him for help.**

Ask for is not used with **to**.

pay   **I paid him the money.**
             I paid for the goods.
             I paid him £100 for the work.

Pay is used without **to** when money is the direct object. It uses **for** with the goods or services bought.

Rewrite the phrases in italics, using an indirect object without **to**, as in the example:

e.g.   *I sent a postcard to John.*
       I sent John a postcard.

Jane   Wonderful news! We're going to get our own house. One of Paul's friends is moving to the north of England and he wanted to *sell his house to us.* Paul *made an offer to him* and he accepted it.

Liz   Did you *give a cheque to him*?

Jane   No! We haven't got all that money. But he *promised the house to us* if we found someone to *lend the money to us.* We *paid a deposit to him* and the building society *guaranteed the rest to us.* Jack *sent a telegram to him* to say it was OK. So all our problems are solved. Of course we *owe a lot of money to the building society*, but we're very happy. Next time you come we'll *show the house to you.*

105   Two-part verbs

Compare these sentences:

Can you **look for** my handbag please?
He's **taken off** his coat. He's **taken** his jacket **off**, too.

Look for and **take off** are two-part verbs. **Look for** is a prepositional verb; it consists of a verb + a preposition. **Take off** is a phrasal verb; it consists of a verb + an adverbial particle.

With prepositional verbs there is only one word order, whether the object is a noun or a pronoun:

verb + preposition + object (noun or pronoun).

With phrasal verbs there are two possible word orders if the object is a noun but only one if it is a pronoun:

verb + preposition + object (noun)
verb + object (noun or pronoun) + preposition.

e.g. **Put up your hands!**
Put your hands up! or **Put them up!** (raise them)
but not: Put up them!
He put up his friend for the night.
He put his friend up for the night. (put someone up meaning 'give someone a bed to sleep in')

Complete these sentences with the two-part verbs in brackets and an appropriate pronoun:

e.g. Can you take all this rubbish and (throw away), please?
Can you take all this rubbish and **throw it away,** please?

1 Artists sometimes draw a pound note on the pavement to see if people will (pick up).
2 I'm afraid this tooth is decayed, Mrs Robinson. I'll have to (take out).
3 I never realised I would enjoy playing golf so much when I (take up).
4 She didn't like her Christmas presents so she (give away).
5 Are you going to wear the shoes, sir, or shall I (wrap up)?
6 He didn't like the job so he (turn down) when they offered it to him. Now a friend of his has offered him one. He has promised to (ring up) tomorrow.
7 The doctor has told me to stop smoking but I haven't enough will-power to (give up).
8 My father says you can (take out) to dinner tonight but you must (bring back) by twelve o'clock.

106 Numerals: **a hundred, hundreds of**

Compare the following:

Three dozen young people came to the concert.
Five hundred young people came to the concert.
Several hundred young people came to the concert.
A thousand young people came to the concert.
Over twenty thousand young people came to the concert.

Dozens of young people came to the concert.
Hundreds of young people came to the concert.
Thousands of young people came to the concert.
Many thousands of young people came to the concert.

Numerals like **dozen, hundred, thousand, million** only take the plural -s ending when we are giving a very vague number, e.g. **hundreds** can mean anything between 200 and 1,000.

Complete the following sentences, using the information given in brackets, and writing the answers in words, not numbers:

e.g. Dinosaurs lived **millions of** years ago. (000,000s).
Dinosaurs lived about **two hundred million** years ago. (200,000,000)

1   He earns _____ pounds a year. (8,000)
2   He earns _____ pounds. (000s)
3   _____ people buy his records. (000,000s)
4   He sold _____ records last year. (5,000,000)
5   The island has _____ inhabitants. (several 100)
6   _____ islanders came to the beach to see us off. (00s)
7   This contract is worth _____ dollars. (over 000,000)
8   This contract is worth _____ dollars. (000,000s)
9   _____ people in the world are suffering from starvation. (Many 000,000s)
10   _____ advisers have been sent by the United Nations to help them to learn better methods of cultivation. (Several 100)
11   I'd like _____ eggs, please. (24: use **dozen**)
12   These hens lay _____ eggs. (12s)

107 **How is . . . ? What is . . . like? What does . . . look like?**

Compare these questions and answers:

A **How is** she?   *B* Oh, she's much better, thanks. Her cold's much better, and the doctor says she can get up tomorrow.

A	**What's** she **like?**	B	She's a rather strange person, but we'll get used to her in time.
			She's very tall, with long, red hair and blue eyes.
			She's getting better at the job. I think she'll be quite an efficient secretary when she gets to know people in the firm.
A	**What does** she **look like?**	B	She's very tall, with long, red hair and blue eyes.

The first question can only refer to the state of health of a person.
The second may ask for a description of someone's personality (or of a thing, a city, a machine, etc.), or for a physical description, or sometimes may ask for an assessment of someone's ability.
The third only refers to physical appearance.

Ask the appropriate questions for the answers given below. Use the third question above for physical description:

1   *A* _____?   *B*   He's not very well, I'm afraid.
2   *A* _____?   *B*   He's a funny little man, with glasses and a beard.
3   *A* _____?   *B*   She's the kindest person I've ever met.
4   *A* _____?   *B*   They work very well. They're much better than the machines we had before.
5   *A* _____?   *B*   They're an odd couple. They're always together but they never seem to say anything to each other.
6   *A* _____?   *B*   Fine. His temperature's back to normal.
7   *A* _____?   *B*   It's round, with an unusual blue-and-white design, and it's made of china, with a surface of enamel.
8   *A* _____?   *B*   It's the most interesting city I've ever been to.

108   **likely** and **probably** (referring to future time)

Compare the use of tenses in these sentences:
They **will probably leave** the hotel.
They **are likely to leave** the hotel.
He **will probably not arrive** on Wednesday.
He **is not likely to arrive** on Wednesday.

Rewrite these sentences, either with **probably** or **likely**, as in the examples above:

1   They'll probably go to England next summer.
2   It's likely to rain tomorrow.
3   The tourist industry will probably grow quite fast next year.
4   The price of hotels will probably go up.
5   The guests will probably receive bad service.

6 They will probably not come back.
7 He is likely to change his mind.
8 They will probably spend more than they can afford.
9 He is not likely to argue.
10 The weather will probably be disappointing.

09 for, during, while

Notice the use of **for**, **during** and **while** in these sentences:

The king was abroad **for three weeks**.
There were street riots **during the king's absence**.
The revolution took place **while the king was away**.

For and **during** are prepositions and are followed by a noun. **For** refers to a total period of time, e.g. **I waited for two hours**. **During** refers to a point of time within a period, e.g. **he died during** (in) **the night**. **While** is a conjunction; it is followed by a clause (subject and verb). It is used to refer to one event taking place at the same time as another.

Complete these sentences with **for**, **during** or **while**:

1 The Hundred Years' War actually lasted _____ over a hundred years.
2 The Hundred Years' War took place _____ the fourteenth and fifteenth centuries.
3 _____ the war was taking place, the Black Death killed a third of the population of Europe.
4 I'm going to give you these pills. They should make you comfortable _____ the night. But if you feel ill _____ the night, call me.
5 He was given the title of Honorary Consul _____ the period of his appointment.
6 _____ he was Consul, he met a lot of interesting people, and he would have liked to stay there _____ another two years, but he became ill _____ the last year of his appointment and had to retire.

110 for, since, ago, from . . . to

Notice the use of **for**, **since**, **ago**, **from . . . to** in these sentences:

He's been learning English **for a long time**.
He's been learning English **since he was a child**.
He started learning English **ten years ago**.
He had English lessons at school **from the age of twelve to the age of eighteen**. Now he's going to evening classes.

Look at the table below and use the information in it to complete the exercises below:

Staff List – Franklin Chemicals Ltd., July 1st, 1981

Name	Joined firm	Previous firm	Position	Time employee there
A. Blake	June 1978	Paul Ltd	accountant	2 years
B. Craig	March 1981	Link Agency	typist	6 months
C. Drake	August 1979	Civil Service	clerk	5 years
D. Ellis	June 1974	Wake Ltd	salesman	a year
E. French	May 1981	Garth & Co	secretary	4 months
J. Grant	June 1975	Browns	accountant	3 years

The personal file for Arthur Blake in July 1981 reads:
He joined the firm in June 1978 so he has been working here for three years. Before that he worked as an accountant for Paul Ltd. **for two years.**
The personal file for Belinda Craig in July 1981 reads:
She joined the firm four months ago. She has been working here since March. Before that she worked as a typist for Link Agency **from September 1980 to March this year.**

1 Rewrite the personal file for Arthur in the same style as the file for Belinda, and rewrite the personal file for Belinda in the same style as Arthur's.

2 Write the files for Drake and Ellis in the same way as the first example about Arthur Blake.

3 Write the files for French and Grant in the same way as the second example about Belinda Craig.

111 **make** and **do**

Look at these sentences:

I have to **make a confession**. I haven't **done my homework**.
She's **done her best**. But she's still **made** a lot of **mistakes**.
I've **made a discovery**. **Doing** one's own car **repairs** can be quite easy.

As a general rule we can say **do** tends to relate to actions, **make** to causing, creating or constructing. However, here is a list of some common expressions, excluding phrasal verbs, for reference:

do

better	an exercise	a job	a service
one's best	a favour	justice (to)	wonders
business	good	a kindness	work

damage	harm	an operation	worse
one's duty	homework	repairs	one's worst
evil	an injury	right	wrong

make

an appointment	an effort	money	a success (of)
arrangements	enquiries	the most (of)	sure (of)
attacks (on)	one's escape	a movement	a trip
the best (of)	an excuse (for)	an offer	trouble (for)
certain (of, about)	faces (at)	peace	use (of)
a change	a fool (of)	preparations	a voyage
a choice	friends (with)	a profit	war (on)
a complaint	fun (of)	progress	way (for)
a confession	a fuss (about)	a report (on, to)	welcome
a decision	a guess	a request	work (for others)
a demand	haste	room (for)	
a difference (to)	a journey	a search (for)	
a discovery	a mistake	a speech	

Complete the exercise without looking at this list. Then check your answers against the list. Use an appropriate form of **do** or **make**:

1.   *A* If you don't _____ an effort, you won't improve your English.
  B Well, I'm _____ my best. I always _____ my homework.
  A Yes, but you _____ too many mistakes. Still I suppose you're _____ some progress.

2. Would you mind _____ me a favour? I've got to _____ a speech on Thursday. I want to _____ certain that it's all right. Would you look at it and _____ any changes you think are necessary. I've never _____ anything like this before and I don't want to _____ a fool of myself. But I think I've _____ justice to the subject.

3.   *A* He's the worst boss I've ever had. He's incapable of _____ a decision, and I'm tired of _____ excuses for him.
  B He means well, though. He doesn't _____ any harm, does he?
  A He doesn't _____ any good, either. I don't know how the company _____ a profit if all their managers are like him. I could _____ his job better myself.

112 **say** and **tell**

a **say** and **tell** with reported statements

Look at these sentences:

    Paul There is a letter for you.
    Paul **said** there was a letter for me.
    Paul **told me** there was a letter for me.

These sentences mean the same, but the uses of the verbs **tell** and **say** are different.

Say means 'speak words'. It has no object.

Tell usually means 'inform a person' and with this meaning always has a personal object (e.g. **me**),

e.g. *Paul* **Hello.**

Paul said hello.

Tell cannot be used. Paul is not giving information. In addition, there is no personal object here.

Tell can have other meanings,

e.g. **He told a story/the truth.** (Here **tell** means 'relate'.)
They're so alike that I can't tell one from another. (Here **tell** means 'distinguish between'.)

Finally, **tell** is used in a special idiom to mean 'read the time from the clock',

e.g. **He's only three. He can't tell the time yet.**

b **say** and **tell** with reported commands

Compare these sentences:

Paul Don't do that again.
Paul **said that I shouldn't** do it again.
Paul **told me not to** do it again.

Note that a reported command with **say** is followed by **that** and the auxiliary **should (not)**. The reported command with **tell** takes an infinitive.

c **say** and **tell**: passive

Note the passive forms:

People say it's a good film.
It's said to be a good film.
People have told me that it's a good film.
I've been told that it's a good film.

Complete these sentences with the correct form of **say** or **tell**:

1 What does the notice _____? I can't read it.
2 This leaflet is supposed to explain the tax system but it doesn't _____ me anything.
3 I'm sorry. I wasn't listening. Did you _____ something?
4 She was _____ me a very interesting story when you came in.
5 You'd better _____ that I'm busy.
6 You'd better _____ them that I'm busy.
7 I've been _____ that there's a lot of trouble at the factory.
8 It's been _____ recently that there's a lot of trouble at the factory.
9 I _____ you not to bet on the numbers. Now we'll lose our money.

10 I _____ don't bet on the numbers. Now we'll lose our money.
11 I can't understand the young people of today. God knows what
    my grandfather would have _____ about your behaviour.
12 I can't understand your behaviour and I don't want to _____
    anything about it. Your grandfather would have _____ you what
    he thought.
13 The instruction _____ that I should report here.
14 I was _____ to report here.
15 *A* The information services of the Government are responsible for
        _____ people how to fill in these forms. When you went to
        the tax office, they must have _____ what to do.
    B They didn't _____ me anything. They just sat there without
        _____ a word.
    A I don't think you're _____ the truth.

13 Alternatives to the reflexive

Compare these sentences:
> I've **cut myself**!
> I've **cut my hand**!

We generally use the reflexive to describe injuries we receive by our
own actions,
e.g. **I hurt myself while I was playing squash.**
      He burned himself with his cigarette.
But we do not use the reflexive if we mention the part of the body,
e.g. **I hit my elbow on the chair.**
      She cut her hand on the edge of the tin.
Where the verb only refers to that part of the body, the reflexive is
impossible,
e.g. **I broke my leg.** (not **myself**)

Complete these sentences with one of the injuries listed below. Use the correct form of the verb
and an appropriate possessive (**my**, **your**, etc.):
e.g. I was lighting the barbecue and **I burned my hand**.
break/leg, burn/mouth, cut/hand, stub/toe, bite/tongue, break/nose,
bang/head, burn/fingers
1 Don't pick up that broken glass! You'll _____.
2 He's so tall that every time he goes through a low doorway, he

   _____.
3 If you touch that hot iron, you'll _____.
4 Almost everyone I know who goes skiing _____ sooner or later.
5 *A* He looks like a boxer.
   B Yes, he _____ when he was young and it didn't set properly.

6 **A** Why are you jumping about on one foot?

  B Who left that heavy box in the doorway? I've _____.

7 That soup's too hot. You'll _____.

8 **A** Ow! I've _____.

  B Well, you shouldn't eat so fast.

114 **so** and **not** to avoid repetition of a clause

Notice the short answers to the questions:

    A Do you think you're going to fail this exam?

    B **I hope I'm not.** (going to fail it)
       I hope not.

Study the lists below, noting where **so** is used in the negative, and where we use **not**, before completing the exercise.

Affirmative	**Negative**
I'm afraid so.	I'm afraid not.
I believe so.	I don't believe so.
I expect so.	I don't expect so.
I hope so.	I hope not.
I imagine so.	I don't imagine so.
I suppose so.	I don't suppose so.
I think so.	I don't think so.

Note that **not** is grammatically acceptable in all negative forms but sounds very formal nowadays, except in **I'm afraid not** and **I hope not**. **I imagine not** is grammatical but very uncommon.

Replace the clauses in italics with **so** or **not**:

1 **A** Do you think life is better than it used to be?

  B Yes, I believe *it is*, at least for most people.

2 **A** Do your students like you?

  B I imagine *they do*.

3 **A** Can you lend me a hundred pounds?

  B I'm sorry. I'm afraid *I can't*.

4 **A** Do you think the cost of living will go down this year?

  B I don't expect *that it will*.

5 **A** Is Mona coming to the party?

  B I don't suppose *she is*. She's very busy.

6 **A** Is her sister coming?

  B I hope *she isn't*. I can't stand her.

Index

Thomas Nelson and Sons Ltd
Nelson House   Mayfield Road
Walton-on-Thames   Surrey KT12 5PL

51 York Place
Edinburgh EH1 3JD

Thomas Nelson (Hong Kong) Ltd
Toppan Building 10/F
22A Westlands Road
Quarry Bay   Hong Kong

Distributed in Australia by

Thomas Nelson Australia
480 La Trobe Street
Melbourne   Victoria 3000
and in Sydney, Brisbane, Adelaide and Perth

© W S Fowler and Norman Coe 1982

First published by Thomas Nelson and Sons Ltd 1982
Reprinted 1983 (twice), 1984, 1985, 1986 (twice),
1987 (twice)

ISBN 0-17-555385-8
NPN 07

Printed in Hong Kong